VISION Paperbacks

DONNA LEIGH-KILE

LAWYERS
ON THE SPOT

First published in Great Britain in 1998 by VISION
Paperbacks, a division of Satin Publications Limited.

VISION Paperbacks,
a division of
Satin Publications Limited
20 Queen Anne Street
London W1M 0AY
E-mail: 100525.3062@compuserve.com

Cover design and layout: Justine Hounam.
Typesetting and design: Pixel Press.
Printed and bound in Great Britain: The Bath Press, Bath.
Photography Rex Features/Press Association/Thom Lafferty

Dedication
To Christian C. Kile.

The Author

*Donna Leigh-Kile began her career as a journalist and fea-
ture writer on local newspapers before joining the London
Evening Standard as a reporter. She has since worked as a
freelance writer in both Britain and the United States for
national newspapers and magazines. She is married with a
son, Christian, and lives in Surrey, England.*

Acknowledgements

I would like to thank all the lawyers in the UK and the US
who contributed either attributably or
unattributably to this book.
This book would not have been possible
without the advice and assistance of: Clive Freedman,
barrister; Dan Soffin, solicitor; Clive Freedman, barrister
and John Steele, crime correspondent, The Daily Telegraph
for background information; Kate Saffett, Gavin Fuller and
James Escarelle-Rees, The Daily Telegraph library; Rhoda
Koenig; Lor Valerie, US researcher; Anthony Bales; Penny
Darbyshire and Ruth Treays.

CONTENTS

THE CAST

UK

Mr. Justice Bell	High Court Judge, conducted the 'Maclibel' trial, the longest case in British legal history, lasting 313 days.
David Bigmore	leading franchise solicitor, David Bigmore & Co.
John Clitheroe	senior partner, Kingsley Napley – major cases: Blue Arrow, Barlow Clowes, BCCI; defended Ian Maxwell.
Jim Edmunds	leading asset finance and leasing solicitor, partner in Beaumont and Son.
Dick Ferguson, QC	leading advocate, defended Rosemary West, Ernest Saunders in the Guinness trial, Birmingham Six appeal.
Sean Gates	foremost aviation solicitor, partner, Beaumont and Son, handled claims which arose from the shooting down of a Korean airliner, 1983.
John Jarvis, QC	Chairman of the Commercial Bar Association 1995 - 1997.
Alun Jones, QC	leading specialist in commercial crime and extradition, defended Kevin Maxwell in the Maxwell Criminal trial.

Lawyers

Caroline Kean	leading media solicitor at Wiggin & Co.
Daphne Loebl	commercial law barrister.
Mike Mansfield, QC	leading defence barrister - major cases: the Brighton Bombings, ABC Official Secrets; the Price Sisters and five of the Birmingham Six.
Sir Brian Neill	retired presiding Lord Justice of Appeal, now sitting as the third Judge on the left wing of the Court of Appeal.
Keith Oliver	partner at Peter & Peters specialising in business crime, defended Kevin Maxwell.
Jacqueline Perry	personal injury barrister, legal expert on BBC radio's 'Jimmy Young' show and ITV's 'Richard and Judy' show.
Richard Sykes, QC	specialist in company law.
Rob Webb, QC	specialist in aviation law.
Arthur Wynn Davies	Legal Manager of the Daily Telegraph.

US

Madelyn Chaber	environmental attorney in California, won landmark $2m case against a tobacco firm for causing her client's cancer.
Henry Hecht	former Assistant Special Prosecutor on the Watergate Special Prosecution force; now author, lawyer and law lecturer at the University of California, Berkeley.
Marvin Mitchelson	leading divorce lawyer, pioneered 'palimony' cases.
John Osborn	leading commercial lawyer and author of 'The Paperchase' and 'The Associates'.
Robert Post	Professor of Law, University of California, Berkeley.

Aspirants

Jim Buchanan	barrister in Jonathan Goldberg, QC's criminal set.
Matthew Reeve	barrister in Rob Webb, QC's civil and commercial set.
Dan Soffin	U.S lawyer and practising U.K solicitor.
Quincy Whitaker	defence barrister in the same set as Helena Kennedy, QC.

Lawyers

Onlookers

Penny Darbyshire	Senior Law Lecturer, Kingston University.
Zoe Etherington	from the office for the Supervision of Solicitors.
Michael Kaplan	barristers' clerk.
Robert Lindsay	City Editor, The Lawyer.
Michael McConville	Professor of Law, University of Warwick.
David Woolfson	recruitment consultant, Chambers & Partners.

Introduction

FAT CATS?

The lawyers' world, which has hardly changed in terms of hierarchy, structure and function since 1340, is being re-engineered, forcing a fundamental overhaul in the way business is handled. A new élite has been created and its members are enjoying enormous financial rewards.

These privileged lawyers, earning up to £1m a year, were recently denounced as 'fat cats' in an extraordinary attack by Lord Irvine, Lord Chancellor and a former eminent practitioner. He said top lawyers could earn up to four times the salary of eminent surgeons, and that the size of their fees deter people from litigation.

But is his attack on fats cats fair? In reality he is rebuking the upper tier of a profession which is dominated by specialist commercial and company lawyers who rarely, if ever, appear in court and who are concerned with global corporate business and litigation. These lawyers make far and away the most money, and their expertise and services are sold all over the world. They work, however, in an area in which the sums at stake are so huge that the percentage taken in legal fees is of minimal importance to the companies who pay them.

Lawyers

But as the fortunes of specialist lawyers wax, the economic circumstances of the vast bulk of the legal profession wane. The abolition of the conveyancing monopoly, long known as the 'bread and butter' fee earner for solicitors, marked the end of middle-class stability and security which they had either taken for granted or expected as their right.

Hundreds of practitioners tried to cling on to their status and standard of living by turning to crime. Such was the scale of it that the Solicitors' Indemnity Fund announced that it will need nearly £1/2 billion more than originally projected to satisfy claims for negligence and dishonesty arising between 1989 and 1997.

Many hundreds more were 'let go' by their firms; cases of bankruptcy soared, and those whose firms survived have often had to accept a dramatic reduction in pay, profits and benefits. According to economist, Jeremy Rifkin, they are part of a new demographic category called the 'declining middle'.

The gap in wages, benefits and morale between lawyers at the top and the rest has therefore never been greater. Frequently compared to the British Football League, there are those in the premier and first divisions of the legal profession who would regard an income of half a million pounds as representing a bad year.

Their US counterparts have still greater earning power and there is more than a sprinkling of dollar billionaires among their number. Such lawyers have been known to retire on what they make on a single deal. They represent part of a new international force, a

Introduction

high-tech nomadic tribe as it has been described. In the pursuit of what their corporate clients demand, lean production, competitive success and market position, they are creating a reassuringly standardised product.

Time has become a critical commodity in this results-oriented culture and has signaled the end of the old-fashioned hierarchical system ruled over by individual barristers. Collaboration and, above all, team work are the order of the day for criminal as well as civil lawyers because decisions are made faster, and shared information leads to fewer mistakes. "You must keep up with the flow of information that requires resolution in a case or you will lose your client, your reputation and ultimately, your job," says one American lawyer.

This team method of working, just one example of the general democratisation of the legal profession, is light years away from the individual élitism, embodied by the self-employed barrister, which has traditionally dominated the top echelons of the law. It favours, instead, the approach of solicitors who have long operated partnerships – one short step away from multi-disciplinary practices, linked up with other professions.

Bluntly put, solicitors now hold the whip hand. Indeed, whilst senior barristers express concern about the continued existence of the Bar as they know it, an increasing number of junior barristers are re-training as solicitors. This would have been virtually unheard of even ten years ago, because the Bar has, until now, always been regarded as the 'senior profession'.

As this book shows, there has always been a division

Lawyers

within the legal profession. It used to be based on class; nowadays there is a polarisation between 'the best and the rest', as a barrister's clerk puts it. It is exacerbated by a widely-held view at the top that only 15 to20 per cent of the entire profession is really good at what it does. The vast majority of lawyers, they believe are, at best, mediocre and, at worst, a waste of money. Some state it openly; others say so in couched terms or off the record. But however it is expressed, it amounts to a damning indictment of 80 per cent of the profession.

While this might dismay and disturb the general public, it will probably not come as a complete surprise. According to Robert Post, Professor of Law at the University of California, Berkeley, lawyers seem to have aroused a special level of animosity from the rest of the population since Biblical times.

Maybe our suspicion of the profession is a consequence of our vulnerability when we find ourselves in the hands of a lawyer. Most of us are so profoundly ignorant of the law and lawyers that we would not be able to distinguish between a good and a bad one until it is too late.

Here then, is a report by an independent, non-legal journalist of what makes the top lawyers tick and what they think about one another, their profession, and you.

Donna Leigh-Kile

Chapter One

SETTING THE SCENE

The classic questions asked of a lawyer are: 'How can you bring yourself to defend a monster like that?' and 'How do you defend someone who is guilty?' All lawyers would answer the first question alike, saying that they are upholding the principle by which everyone accused of a crime deserves the right to representation in court. "Whether or not you are disgusted by your client or the alleged crime, you are not doing your job unless those are irrelevant considerations," says barrister Quincy Whitaker. "You are not the jury. You are the mouthpiece for your client. You are saying what he would say had he completed a law degree and been trained at the Bar. I don't think you can rationalise it in any other way.

"It's not about justice and doing the right thing because sometimes you feel your client is probably guilty and ought to get a long sentence for it. But it's wrong, if not impossible to do your job on any other basis than 'I am a representative of what my client says'."

It is a stance the public finds unnatural as it runs counter to their innate sense of common justice. And it lies at the root of why many people believe lawyers,

Lawyers

"manipulate the legal system without any concern for right and wrong," which is the main reason they give for specifically disliking lawyers.*

Nowhere is this more clearly demonstrated than when a lawyer represents a universally hated figure such as Myra Hindley, or more recently, Rosemary West. Dick Ferguson, QC, in his role as West's leading counsel highlights the extraordinarily disturbing position of a trial lawyer. Though we know he is only representing the interests of his client and that his words may not reflect his own views, to run a successful defence it is vital that he convinces us he is sincere.

That entails becoming inextricably associated with his client's viewpoint and in the highly emotive case of Rosemary West, it was inevitable that some of the public identified Ferguson with his client and were intensely hostile. During the trial the QC was subjected to hate mail full of "vitriol and contempt" whose writers were, he says, "either ignorant or unmindful of the fact that I was discharging a public duty."

In addition, he had to sit through, test and assimilate the mass of horrendous evidence impassively or else risk seeing his client's case damaged by a single look of shock or horror. "Throughout, you have to present the appearance that somehow it does not impact on you as a human being. You have to appear devoid of human reaction or revulsion. The juror can bow his head or hide her face. For us there is no such escape. The media

* What America really thinks about lawyers, National Law Journal, 1986.

watch with heightened interest to search for any sign of weakness. It all adds to the tension," he recalls in an article he wrote for the Inner Temple magazine.

PROTECTING THE GUILTY?

The answer to the second question about how lawyers defend the guilty is two-pronged. "If a person says 'I'm guilty'," says Mike Mansfield, QC, "you say, 'then plead guilty and I can mitigate for you'. I may think someone is guilty who tells me he is not but that's beside the point. Unfortunately, people get the idea from novels and TV that you know your client is guilty but you make up a defence for him or get him off on a technicality. That's absolutely not true. If it were so, I'd just as soon leave the profession."

But there is more to it than that. Dick Ferguson, QC explains: "A more difficult situation, and the one I think the public does have a great deal of trouble understanding, is what happens when someone tells you he did it but does not plead guilty. I am not allowed to call that person to the witness box and let him say he is innocent. But I am entitled to represent him, to enter a plea of 'not guilty' and then say to the prosecution, 'Prove your case.' The aim of the exercise is proving the case, not discovering the truth."

Clients' interests though, are not always paramount in the eyes of the legal profession. The lawyer is bound to abide by certain professional rules and if these happen to conflict with the needs and desires of his client, the client may well be the loser. Barrister Jacqueline Perry

Lawyers

recalls: "I was once opposing a very experienced personal injury lawyer who found a case which was dead against him and, instead of quietly ignoring it, he drew it to the judge's attention. He lost the case – not because of that – but it certainly didn't help his cause. People might say, 'But is it proper he does this at the expense of his client?' And the answer is yes, because you owe a duty to the court."

Understandably, the public who feel deep down that law and justice ought to be one-and-the-same blame the practitioners. Hence the age-old tradition of lawyer bashing. St. Luke says in the New Testament: "Woe unto you also, ye lawyers! for ye lade men with burdens grievous to be borne..." and Sir Thomas More banned them from his Utopia. But in defence of their kind, Ferguson says: "There is always bound to be a gap between law and justice because the legal system is a human system complete with human imperfections. Those who administer the law, however, should be striving all the time to reduce that gap." And Rob Webb, QC, says: "Law tries to embody justice – sometimes it succeeds, sometimes it doesn't – but they have always been different concepts."

Being a lawyer is a naturally antagonistic occupation in Britain and the US as we share an adversarial system comprising two opponents, prosecutor and defence, arguing the case before an umpire, the judge.

"It's perhaps too accusatorial. It's like hot-rod racing, where you drive against each other and wait and see if one of you swerves," says Webb. "I think the legal establishment is doing what it can to avoid that because it's not a system which has found favour in a lot of other countries. In Japan, for instance, it has never been adopted.

"Here we are seeing a greater search for consensus with the promotion of tribunals concerned with mediation, conciliation and arbitration. I think this process will go on and there will be less head-to-head combat. But one can't overlook the fact that sometimes people don't want their disputes resolved. What they want is a bit of head-to-head combat and there has to be an outlet in a civilised society for people who want to fight. They are too old for boxing and I'm not sure it is healthy to give them both cushions and tell them to go off and play – so they need the legal system. I like to think I can do what my client wants. If he wants a fight, I can give him a fight. If he wants conciliation, I can give him conciliation."

In Japan, however, where to sue is socially shameful and a failure to reach agreement is a disgrace, the judge plays an active mediating role in an attempt to persuade the two sides to accept a compromise settlement. Solicitor Sean Gates says: "There is a protracted period of negotiation and a case may take as long as four to five years to settle which we would find very frustrating. But despite the lengthy time scale, a case would not necessarily cost more because it is not so intensive."

RAMBO PLAN

American divorce lawyer Marvin Mitchelson observes that lawyers fall into two basic personality types – the aggressor and the conciliator. By his own definition he is tough. "If people co-operate with me, we seem to get on well. I'm only hard on them when they're not fair to their wives. I like to proceed the easy way. I'm not an ogre out to wreck people."

Nonetheless, when actress Joan Collins filed for divorce from her fourth husband, Peter Holm, Mitchelson's ruthlessness was evident in his implementation of what he described as the 'Rambo plan'. Over one weekend, he obtained the necessary restraining orders preventing her husband from coming near her children and from entering her new home. He also had security men remove the few clothes Holm had installed to establish his presence there, and had all the locks changed on the doors. Holm was then handed the keys to the family home that he and the actress had shared during their brief marriage.

Mitchelson also insists upon his clients accepting his command. "I set certain ground rules which they have to follow or I'm useless to them as a lawyer. The main rule is not to negotiate for themselves."

While trial lawyers in the US tend, in the main, to become either prosecutors or defenders, in Britain advocates pride themselves on being able to do both. "One of the advantages of our system," says barrister Jacqueline Perry, "is that we are expected to prosecute a case one day and co-defend in the next, so we retain impartiality." This principle of non-discrimination is enshrined in what lawyers call the 'cab rank rule'. Barristers are supposed, in theory, to take on every case offered them within their specialist field unless they are already involved in a case.

Setting the Scene

The rule, however, is followed more in the breach than the observance, as one leading QC explains: "I would find an excuse if, say, a major case I am in is settled early and I am offered a lesser case in Northampton. I would rationalise it this way; although I may not have any conflicting commitments now, I soon would have – from people offering me work that I regard as more demanding or calling on my particular specialist skills."

A radical junior barrister says: "We can always excuse ourselves from a case by saying we haven't the time or we are not senior enough. Certainly, I would be too busy to represent a National Front member. But such a problem doesn't tend to arise because we are usually briefed by solicitors who share our views. Ignoring the cab rank rule also goes on in establishment sets (the name for barristers' offices). I know they take privately paid cases over legal aid cases."

There is also the added complication of how the barrister is perceived by those who hire him. Alun Jones, QC who defended Kevin Maxwell says: "When I am asked to prosecute, I prosecute. When I am asked to defend, I defend. But I am asked to defend a lot more because I am able to defend vigorously and, therefore, the prosecution tends to distrust me a bit."

Specialisation has thus resulted in certain individual barristers and sets of chambers gaining a reputation for prosecuting and others for defending. However, lawyers who want to select and categorically state the kind of cases they will do and will not do on the grounds of conscience, are often criticised for violating a basic tenet

Lawyers

of the English legal system.

One such practitioner, Mike Mansfield, QC is unmoved. He says he specialises in cases touching upon civil liberty issues in much the same way other barristers specialise in tax or planning law and, although he is described as a radical defence barrister, he does also prosecute. "Furthermore, I think a barrister should be able to refuse a case if he has a serious, genuine, legitimate conscientious objection for doing so. For instance, he refuses to defend in a terrorist case because his family were bomb victims or, classic case, he is a Jewish lawyer confronted with defending a racist dedicated to the eradication of the Jewish race."

TAKING SIDES

Although lawyers in the United States accept there is a place for a 'hired gun', or a 'mouthpiece in criminal law', they regard this as exceptional. Taking sides is the norm, and conscience may play a large part in a lawyer's choice of case. It is virtually unknown, says Californian attorney, Madelyn Chaber, who recently won a $2 million victory against a tobacco company for causing her client's cancer, that an environmental litigator like herself would switch over to the other side and defend, say, a corporation charged with causing pollution.

Another US lawyer has no qualms about stating his reasons for not wanting to be a defence attorney. "I just could not see myself defending people who are accused of crimes when many of them are guilty, especially now that I am a doting dad. It does not appeal to my personal sense of the way things should work in the world. I don't agree with the theory that, even though you may let the guilty go free, all society can feel safe because the state has gone through due process of law."

Notions of winning and losing are equally divergent. Ferguson, QC says: "What is never mentioned is that many cases, irrespective of the abilities of the advocates, are going to come out the same way. The number of cases in which the unique skill of one advocate as against another makes a difference is very small indeed. That's bad for business but it's true. Obviously, you can play a losing hand with great skill but it still remains a losing hand. That's not the fault of the player playing the losing hand, it's just the way the cards are dealt."

Or as Webb, QC says: "Whilst winning or losing can become a matter of skill, it can also become a matter of luck. It rather depends whose brief lands on your desk."

Aviation solicitor Sean Gates objects to the civil legal system itself which he says, "is designed for the entertainment and pleasure of the legal profession rather than with the swift and economic resolution of disputes. The system allows a distinct élite to play an intellectual game with each other. It really doesn't matter to them who wins or loses because that's just a consequence of the game. It's the game that is important. It's not satisfactory that they should be indulging their intellects at the expense of commerce."

Indeed, lawyers fall easily into game terminology when describing their profession. Barrister Matthew Reeve says: "Personally, it is very fulfilling - I can argue to my heart's content. I love it. You play a game to fairly defined rules and, if you do it efficiently, at the same time advance your client's case." They like the challenge of games with high stakes and are well-pleased by the recognition and approval from their peers as well as the financial reward that comes with victory.

WINNING ACCLAIM

Criminal lawyers are no different from their colleagues in wanting to win for the sake of their own professional reputation. "To be brutally honest, the commitment involved in doing defence work is not just to the client – there is also one's own ego, one's desire to do the best job possible and to win the acclaim of one's peer group," says Ferguson.

"But first and foremost, you do think about the client and the horrendous consequences of losing: the ten, fifteen years, life imprisonment. Emotionally you pour yourself into a case – and I'm sure I'm not unique - you try to permeate the jury with your conviction and use all skills you possess to secure an acquittal for your client. While you are waiting for a verdict you are absolutely churned up inside and when the result comes out, you just feel drained. If the jury convicts after you have given the case your all, your immediate reaction is, 'stuff you.'

"But then you go away and come to terms with it: you think about the evidence and the victims."

Civil lawyers like John Jarvis, QC, Chairman of the Commercial Bar Association have no verdicts and sentences to give them nightmares. "While it is obviously a pleasure to win, I am not someone who feels any great disappointment in losing so long as I know I have done my job well. But it is easy for me because most of my clients tend to be big corporations – and we are talking big litigation, where it is my clients' balance sheets that are at stake, not their personal pockets.

"My clients come to me because they want money or some commercial advantage and they do not like it sometimes when I tell them that they cannot win. I am bound to spell out a client's prospects but should he insist on going on with the case despite what I have told him, I will say things like: 'I will fight this for you and give it my best shot. But remember you are the sort of person who pays my children's school fees. We love clients like you'."

Wanting to win too much is more likely to happen when acting for individuals. It is a risk solicitors are more prey to than barristers, says Jarvis, since their job requires them to be close to the client.

"Once you get too close to the client and want too much to win for him then, it seems

Sean Gates, aviation specialist

Lawyers

to me, you begin to lose your judgment."

Media solicitor Caroline Kean views it differently. "I go in every time wanting to win and, whether it's self-delusion or not, passionately believing in my case. But winning to me is improving my client's position. Say the client is faced with paying an aggrieved plaintiff £100,000 but I get him out on a deal of £20,000 quickly, cleanly and cheaply. That is real success, and he goes away happy. In essence, winning means winning in the client's terms: to recover some money, not to give an apology, or to protect a reputation."

Since lawyers are employed to do battle on behalf of others, it is hardly surprising that they are perceived to be a litigious bunch when dealing with personal matters. "It can be a nuisance when you are dealing with policemen, surveyors and architects because they run for cover and won't give you any sort of categorical advice," says one. They assume that we'll take them to court if there are any differences."

Lawyers insist , however, that they do not love litigation for its own sake. Barrister Matthew Reeve says: "We know how much of a hassle it is. I tell my family never to sue unless the case has an overriding principle that is interesting enough to keep their attention for two years or is worth more than £10,000."

He adds: "We are litigation brokers. We play poker for other people."

Chapter Two

THE CHARACTERS

The legal species in Britain has long been divided by sex, race and above all class. The profession is also divided into solicitors, who prepare a client's case, and barristers who plead the case, and the relationship between these two sub-species, like the legal system itself, is adversarial. It can and does degenerate into subversive warfare, akin to a sparring match between boxers who 'psych' themselves up by doing each other down – in the full knowledge that they need each other to function.

On an individual level, the successful solicitor-barrister relationship may be a far cry from this. Some are so well-matched that their wit, timing, virtuosity and preparation put them on a par with ice skaters Torvill and Dean. However, the two profession are wary of one another, understandably as we shall see.

Solicitors are usually thought of as general legal advisers, accessible to the public. A common analogy made is that they play GP to the barrister's consultant although, in many instances, they have become specialists, and a 1991 survey showed they considered themselves as such. Barristers earn their living by presenting civil and criminal cases in court or to a judge and, when acting professionally, are known as 'counsel'.

Quite a number, however, have specialised in a particular branch of the law to such a degree that they rarely appear in courts. When consulted by solicitors – professional etiquette precludes them from dealing directly with lay clients – they give written advice on legal matters, which is known as 'taking counsel's opinion'.

Barristers believe that theirs is the higher-status profession. "Both sides feel that," says one. "Sometimes it is a bit of a barrier between us." They also maintain that they are intellectually superior to their solicitor colleagues – a belief widely held even among law students today. "There is no doubt that the first-class brains are to be found at the Bar rather than in a solicitor's office," says a law graduate.

Traditionally, barristers have always been 'one step removed' from the actual client (though this may change) and they take great pride in upholding the disinterested, objective view. Explains one barrister: "The solicitor is close to the client. The closer he is, the better for business but sometimes someone is needed who hasn't got such a personal investment in the case. Someone who can, for example, give the unwelcome news that the judge won't share the client's point of view, or offer objective specialist advice at a turning point in a case."

This fair and detached observation belies surprisingly vicious swipes by barristers at solicitors who, after all, are their clients. "Because of solicitors' direct relationship with the client they are more susceptible to committing fraud or embezzling client funds," said one brief unattributably. "We face the embarrassing dilemma of being asked by solicitors to withhold from the court information that is damaging to the lay client's case, which the client has let slip despite being advised by his solicitor not to mention it. They know we are legally bound to enter it into court."

One barrister cites as an example the lay client who, seeking damages for personal injuries, reveals either that they are moonlighting, or have declared lower earnings in their tax returns and want the true loss of income to be taken into account when calculating their compensation.

AN ATTITUDE PROBLEM

Bluntly put, the solicitor stereotype which emerges from these barristers' comments is of a lawyer who has fewer grey cells than his learned colleagues; is on occasion too close to his clients, following the clients' wishes and bending the rules to satisfy those wishes; and, most damning of all, prone to criminal avarice.

Richard Sykes, QC and a leading expert in company law, says: "The attitudes that some of my barrister colleagues adopt towards solicitors horrify me.

"They regard solicitors as stupid, second-class citizens and if anything goes wrong they blame the solicitors rather than themselves or their own colleagues. This attitude, however, is built into our legal tradition, because there is no doubt that historically solicitors were seen as third-class citizens."

Lawyers

Sykes, who is descended from a long line of lawyers (his grandfather, aunt and uncles were solicitors and his father was a barrister) says that one of the most marked changes he has observed in his 38 years of practising law is the quality and level of work done by solicitors. "Truthfully, in a specialist field like mine, the major solicitors' firms have quite as much expertise as anybody at the Bar except, of course, in advocacy."

While the stereotype of the intellectually superior barrister arose from a class division, what credibility it has nowadays at the top of the profession is mainly derived from a status divide, increasingly defined by academic excellence. "A first from Oxford or Cambridge is not an 'open sesame' but we do still regard it as a true mark of ability," says John Jarvis, QC. "If someone comes from one of the new universities (previously polytechnics) and claims a first from one of those, we know it does not have the same meaning, frankly. I am not unmindful of the fact that there are late developers, or people who have the ability but do not get in because of capricious and unfair circumstances but, by and large, we feel that with a good Oxbridge degree, the first sifting of candidates has been done for us."

Rob Webb, QC argues: "I think the downside of this emphasis on academic ability is that you tend to get people at the Bar who are too clever, too young. Graduates with firsts, two or even three degrees, tend to be chosen and they tend to wither when faced with real people fighting real situations. As for barristers thinking they are brighter than solicitors, there is no intellectual basis for it that I can understand. The Bar exams are as easy as the solicitors' exams, in fact easier, I think. I would not have thought that your average litigation solicitor would regard his barrister as intellectually superior. He might be jealous that a barrister does not have partners, keeps more of what he earns and has more glamour in court.

"But equally, a barrister might be envious of the security a partnership gives, of a solicitor's ability to delegate the boring bits of work to others, or the fact that if business slumped his firm might be supported by the Pensions or Mergers and Acquisitions Departments. A successful solicitor won't be at all envious of an only moderately successful barrister."

Another leading barrister goes further. "There are barristers who do think they are intellectually superior but, they are not those at the top. They tend to be of a certain age and not very successful. I can actually think of one who is a complete failure as a barrister yet still talks of solicitors almost as if they were the scum of the earth. It's ridiculous."

MUTUAL CONTEMPT

Successful solicitors, however, no longer labour under a collective inferiority complex as they did as recently as ten or fifteen years ago. These days, equality based on mutual contempt has been achieved. They now verbally retaliate with rapier-like precision, or worse. Solicitor Sean Gates says: "There is a snobbery which exists against solicitors based on class and intellectual prejudices. I do believe that the class system still operates at the Bar. You will not find many QCs who are the sons of coal-miners. They will, in the main, have come from families able to subsidise them at university and throughout their training and who have connections which enable them to move up.

"Every country has its own system for the advancement of the élite. Ours is the class system. No group which has achieved this sort of advancement, success, position, power and authority is going to give it up easily. Why should they? And pushed, they will play dirty, hence their comments about solicitors putting their hands in the till. In any group there are going to be a few bad eggs, be they solicitors, barristers or judges."

Media solicitor, Caroline Kean, says: "This is very controversial but of those at the Bar there are only 20% , maybe, for whom I have any respect. And for those barristers I have a very great respect. They can make or break a case and earn every penny they make. But I believe that 80% of the Bar are living in an ivory tower. There is still a tendency, usually amongst general practitioners rather than specialists, to think, 'I'm the barrister, you are the solicitor – so shut up and listen', even though I might know more about the particular matter under discussion than they do. I experienced a lot of this in the past and it still goes on."

Kean, who made partner at 27, says her position and experience ensure that she no longer experiences such patronising behaviour. "Frankly, if it did, I would terminate working with that barrister and go to somebody else.

The Characters

Like many solicitors, I use a few barristers whom I trust. I may have worked with them before or seen them in action, or they come highly recommended by colleagues who know me and how I operate. The barristers I respect most are those who work with me as a team."

Keith Oliver, a partner in the specialist criminal firm Peter & Peters, concurs. "I would not encourage working with barristers who are party to holier-than-thou, self-righteous attitudes which one sometimes comes across in the hallowed precincts of the Temple or Lincoln's Inn. Some cling to a type of Victorian idyll that they are some-how above the fray and belong to an élite club. For instance, there is something called counsel-to-counsel discussions to which solicitors are not as of right invited. What happens is that barristers on opposing sides go off for an informal exchange on how to carve up a case, or to discuss certain issues and then report back to us, their client solicitors.

"In my experience such discussions can destructively erode the barrister-solicitor relationship. They fuel the belief that there are intellectual and philosophical differ-ences between solicitors and barristers, so that it can appear to the lay client that his barrister is closer to the opposing barrister than to the solicitor on his own side which is very odd, given that it is the opposition who is making the client's life a misery."

These 'barristers only' meetings often go on at the criminal Bar, says Oliver, although the days are gone when solicitors were, without exception, excluded from barristers' discussions with the judge. "You have to be

Lawyers

flexible about these things because there are times when such chats are useful," he says. "But any barrister who works for our firm is normally discouraged from engaging in any counsel-to-counsel discussions unless we are present."

Elite lawyers apart, the normal solicitor-barrister relationship at, say, magistrates and Crown Court level, remains as unequal as ever, according to law professor Michael McConville, an author of 'Standing Accused', based upon a study of nearly fifty firms of solicitors. "In my experience solicitors are intimidated by even the most junior members of the Bar. They are highly deferential towards them, will not act without their advice and usually will not challenge their advice.

"The normal relationship is one in which the most junior barrister will be able to exercise an absolute control over the case and, indeed, act in a way which for the most part ignores the advice of the solicitor. Because of this, it encourages solicitors to keep away.

"It is very rare, in my view, for solicitors in any way to exercise influence over the behaviour of barristers. Even though the behaviour of barristers is clearly open to criticism, censure, or worse, none of those things will occur, because of the difference in the power relationship. Indeed, solicitors will cover for barristers."

McConville accepts junior barristers' arguments that all too often they end up having a hurried five-minute conference in court with the defendant because they have inadequate information about the case they are about to conduct. For instance, a junior barrister represented eight defendants he had never previously met, without any instructions at all and, when not in court, was in the cells seeking instruction directly from the clients. He was paid £70 for the day's work.

According to many solicitors and even some barristers, the separation of legal power, which has existed for the past 650 years, is not only unnecessary but doomed. They predict that barristers as a separate sub-species will eventually become extinct. "From an international perspective, barristers are almost irrelevant and nationally they cling on to their dominance with the aid of the judicial system," says solicitor Sean Gates. "I think their pomposity or grandeur is a form of self-defence. I don't think it is necessary to have a separate Bar as there is much more written work in court work now and much less call for advocacy talent. Theatrics are almost dead."

Mike Mansfield, QC, agrees with Gates that the existing Bar "is going to wither and die," although he believes there will always be a need for an independent stream of lawyers

Mike Mansfield, QC

Lawyers

specialising in advocacy. "Lawyers will become consultants whether they like it or not. Having to compete in an open market, driven by economics, there won't be enough work to keep the Bar going as a separate entity. The barrister's profession as a whole is failing. The structure of it is crazy, the entry to it is crazy – and I think it's going to die on its feet. It has fought the wrong battles in the past, looked backwards instead of forwards, and dug its heels in. I think we should have one legal profession, as they do in other parts of the world."

Whilst Mansfield may be in a minority in wanting fusion, many more of his colleagues reluctantly accept it as inevitable in the long term. For several years, there has been ever-increasing interbreeding between the two branches of the profession – and secondary characteristics, as well as some primary ones, have been crossing species lines. Since 1990 solicitors have extended rights of advocacy at Crown Court level, and a number of solicitor-advocates have rights to appear in the High Court.

Some territorial markings have been preserved though: barristers and solicitors are required to dress formally when appearing in a court case. For a barrister this entails wearing a wig and gown, without which he cannot be 'seen' or 'heard' by the judge. He may look as if he has wandered in from a medieval mystery play but the fancy dress nevertheless distinguishes him from ordinary human clay. Solicitors must wear a gown but are not allowed to wear wigs. Lord Taylor, the late Lord Chief Justice, failed in his attempt two years ago to abolish wigs and gowns after a consultation exercise brought heavy opposition from judges, barristers, jurors and the public. But the greatest opposition to change in past surveys has been from defendants and witnesses.

Unexpectedly, the pressure to give solicitors greater rights of audience is not coming only from their side. "A number of leading barristers say that a proportion of our side of the profession is inadequate," says an eminent establishment QC. "What the proportion is, I don't know, but I certainly agree. For that reason, I have been supporting the former Lord Chancellor's reforms which allow solicitor advocacy. It seems to me that's the only way we are going to sharpen up the act of some of the people who have had it much too good for too long."

One High Court judge who has heard three cases conducted by solicitor-advocates thinks they are "jolly good." "You hear colleagues say they are awful but they just as frequently say they've had an awful barrister in front of them."

David Woolfson, of Chambers & Partners Legal Recruitment Consultants, says that city firms such as Clifford Chance, Herbert Smith and S J Berwin & Co., are building up their solicitor advocacy departments, and a few others are considering doing the same. The fear amongst barristers is that by employing their own full-time advocates, firms of solicitors will squeeze out all but the top rank of specialist barristers. Furthermore, the 'big boy' solicitors' firms will have a monopoly on the most able advocates by wooing them away from their self-employment status with irresistible salaries and bonuses.

"The brightest and best young graduates would be

snapped up by big city firms like Freshfields, and Slaughter and May – and it would mean that the medium and small-sized solicitors' firms which could never afford their own advocacy departments could be at a grave disadvantage. They would have access to a Bar diminished not only in size but in ability," speculates one top commercial QC. My own son graduates from Cambridge this year and he intends becoming a solicitor-advocate."

A 29-year-old barrister who is re-training as a solicitor says three of his contemporaries are doing the same. "I don't think the Bar is going anywhere – and I'd much rather be with solicitors moving up the ladder than with barristers who are moving down."

To be a barrister, one must belong to one of the four Inns of Court: Gray's Inn, Lincoln's Inn, Inner Temple and Middle Temple. When this barrister notified his Inn that he intended becoming a solicitor he was told he ought to disbar himself. He discovered, however, that it was not compulsory and, when he finally qualifies as a solicitor, he hopes to obtain dual status which will mean he can continue using the Inns' legal library and dining halls.

Mergers between solicitors' firms and barristers' chambers may be round the corner, a measure which would, of course, give barristers more security but also deprive them of their independence. At an individual level more transfers are also taking place. One top commercial barrister says he is seriously considering crossing over: "I can retain my title as QC. I can sell my goodwill to a partnership. I can build up a string of lawyers under me to do the work." Whilst it is possible to be doubly qualified, no one is allowed to practise as a barrister and solicitor at the same time.

The Bar is currently more concerned about what impact an increasing use of solicitor-advocates in less important cases will have on the younger members of the Bar . "How are my juniors going to get experience," asks more than one barrister, "if clients feel that a barrister is necessary only when there is more than X pounds at issue?"

The prevailing image of the legal profession as a service industry and the Bar's increasingly tenuous place in it, combined with the recession a few years ago, are major reasons barristers have shed much of their aloofness.

Solicitor Keith Oliver observes: "Now we are invited to a plethora of cocktail parties at the Bar and to in-house seminars where we can hear barristers with expertise in a particular field speaking on it for three-quarters of an hour, over a glass of wine. Of itself, this isn't spreading knowledge for the benefit of the legal community; it's done simply to generate work. To survive and compete they have become much more hard-nosed."

John Jarvis, QC agrees that the Bar is much more accessible these days. As for it resembling an exclusive club, he says: "I think that was probably right twenty years ago, but now when I have conferences with solicitors, rather than delivering my opinion to them on tablets of stone, we have a dialogue. I would also dispute the idea that we are divorced from real life. As one judge said, 'I go to the supermarket.' Like many others, I've done work in which I've had to deal with very poor, desperate families, fights in public houses and so forth."

Criminal solicitor John Clitheroe, senior partner at the firm of Kingsley Napley, recalls a time when it was against the rules for barristers to associate with solicitors. "The Bar was not allowed to socialise, lunch with, have drinks with, or...or fraternise with solicitors — and distinction between the Bar and the solicitors was very carefully kept. It was thought to be against their dignity, that it might compromise their independence, or even be seen as touting for business. It meant that a solicitor and barrister in the same case were prevented from having lunch together."

SOCIAL SEPARATION

Many senior lawyers still smart at the memory of having to sit at a separate table from their barrister colleagues. "They belonged to a different social strata. The solicitor was the journeyman lawyer and the barrister the élite specialist," says Clitheroe. "In the late 1950's, we approached Counsel almost in the guise of a supplicant because we were brought up to believe that barristers were matchless, the nonpareil of the legal profession. "

Clitheroe remembers how much controversy was stirred up when solicitor David Napley, who was representing the former Liberal Party leader Jeremy Thorpe, consulted with George Carman, QC, who was due to appear in the trial, on the strategy at the committal proceedings.

The Characters

"Many members of the Bar regarded George Carman's discussion with a solicitor on how to conduct part of the case before he was officially involved as a betrayal - a breach of protocol of the Bar. And there was great resentment among some people against both George and David. The difference between 1970 and 1997 is that leading QCs ask solicitors to come and see them as early as possible so they can discuss tactics and work as a team from the start."

Even so, leading solicitors in their 30's and early 40's admit to having suffered bouts of servile behaviour at the start of their careers. "When I was an articled clerk," says one, "I was very intimidated by the mere presence of counsel. Metaphorically, I was almost raising my hand to speak," said one.

In contrast, and in the interests of 'perceived classlessness and upward mobility', the US decided in favour of a unified Bar, says Robert Post, a Professor of Law at the University of California, Berkeley. "We decided to define ourselves against the English system so there is no formal division between barristers and solicitors. There are, nonetheless, major status distinctions which are unofficial, informal but very powerful within the American Bar. For example, members of élite corporate law firms have a very different status as well as lifestyle, income and access to judges and resources from that of solo practitioners.

"Historically, status had to do with race: the old Anglo-Saxon practitioners versus new immigrant practitioners. Nowadays, this is less so. It has more to do with the nature of the firm and its clientele."

Clearly then, although its nature may alter with time or differ according to geography and culture, there will always be an élite whatever else may become extinct within the legal profession.

PORTIA AND HER KIND

"In the practice of law, women are natural guerrilla fighters. I believe that there are differences in the psyches of men and women, and consequently, women are capable of a more adroit handling of a set of rules, which is why it is amazing that men have been able to keep them out for so long," says aviation solicitor, Sean Gates.

Leading media solicitor Caroline Kean agrees: "I see more and more women litigators these days who are better than men precisely because of their female qualities. When they fight for their clients, they have a kind of single-mindedness and ruthlessness of a mother cat fighting for her kittens."

Still often regarded as an unknown quantity by their male counterparts, they can turn this to their distinct advantage. "They don't know what I am going to do," says one senior female solicitor, "I can play anything from 'Doris Day' to the 'bitch from hell', whatever serves my purpose, although I much prefer playing the bitch from hell."

Another says: "There is a tendency to underestimate us - and that can prove very costly for the opposing lawyer and his client. One essential difference between our psyches and theirs is that they feel they cannot lose face, and that prevents them learning from their mistakes."

Women, in general, are less likely to assume that their charm and flair will see them through, and are more likely to scrutinise every aspect of their case, hence the stereotype of the head-down, earnest female lawyer.

"When I was a pupil," says a successful female barrister, "I would come back from court and analyse what I had done and what I should have done. My pupil master would say, 'But did you win?' and I'd say, 'Oh, yes'. The reaction was bewilderment that I should still be going over the case. But I felt that simply winning wasn't enough – I could have done better."

There are some 30,000 women in the UK who are qualified as solicitors but curiously, no exact statistics on how many of them actually practise. The total number of female barristers and advocates in the UK is somewhere in the region of 2,000 although again, no one seems to know what percentage practise. What is known is that more than half the trainees and new solicitors are women, and that lately they have been obtaining more first-class degrees and higher grades in the Law Society training course than men. Yet only 20% of new partners in the top 30 firms are women, and in the top 100, only 14%.

The poor showing by female barristers is more easily explained. Until 1990 it was quite legal for sets of chambers to ban women because barristers, being self-employed, were exempt from the Sex Discrimination Act of 1975. Shamefully, when the senate of the Bar was asked if there should be a clause in the Act to make it apply to the granting of a position in chambers - the vote was a resounding no.

The legal loophole may have been closed seven years ago but the territorial attitudes did not vanish with a stroke of the pen. Occasional examples of harassment come to light and may result in disciplinary proceedings. A few years ago, a QC was suspended for three months after complaints were made against him, but this rare.

One senior solicitor in his late 40's, confides that some barristers of his generation regard the selection of pupils (female trainees) as 'a perk of the job'. "You will find that a lot of young female pupils are tall, blonde, and blue-eyed with 'certain attributes', because that's what the boys like. Whether they get beyond pupillage (on-the-job training) is another story."

Quincy Whitaker was suspicious when she was offered a pupillage by one highly-rated criminal set of chambers, despite the undemanding nature of her interview "I was asked what I had seen at the theatre and cinema. Very little was asked about the law at all. Then they offered me a pupillage and I didn't see how they could possibly have assessed me properly, or taken me seriously on the basis of that interview. I saw later that they offered quite a lot of their pupillages to young women, yet they had only two women tenants." *

*barristers who have earned a permanent place in chambers.

Summing up the problems which can face young female barristers, she says: "It is not unknown for QCs and senior members of chambers to make advances to pupils, who are in a completely invidious position. You are damned if you do, and damned if you don't. If you say yes, there's no guarantee you will be given a permanent position in chambers; if it is no, you certainly won't."

Invidious distinctions between the sexes do not necessarily stop once a woman is taken on by a set of chambers. She may not be allocated her fair proportion of work by the clerks, or it may be less remunerative than that of her male colleague. They can find themselves on an unremitting diet of 'women's interest' cases, such as rape, harassment and assault.

Solicitors sometimes do not want a woman, and clients will also make their preferences known. Whitaker, who was assigned to defend an East Ender charged with hijacking a cigarette lorry, recalls: "When I walked in, he said, 'I've got a bird'. I told him he was perfectly free to sack me if he wanted to be represented by a man. He apologised and we got on with the case. But when I asked him to repeat certain conversations, he would bleep out all the swear words, saying, 'I never swear in front of a lady.' There are clients who will shoot someone in the kneecaps, but they won't swear in front of a lady. It seems a rather odd moral code."

Female barristers agree, however, that it is much less of a struggle for them than it was for their predecessors. "We have five women in these chambers but, when I joined, there was just one, and she was the first. Imagine the isolation," says another barrister. "I think I knew in theory what the difficulties would be in joining a man's world like the Bar but I had no idea what the effects would be. When I got my tenancy, I felt I had arrived where I belonged. Now there are parts of myself which don't belong here at all. There is a conflict between being a good wife and mother and being a good barrister."

And herein lies the greatest practical obstacle to female participation in the law at its highest levels. "I have a great deal of respect for women lawyers," says the head of a leading firm of solicitors. "But I think they are setting themselves a tremendous problem trying to run a business and a home at the same time. It is as if I tried to be both a lawyer and an architect.

"I had a woman solicitor who was superbly qualified and very good at her job. I came in one day and found her in tears because she just couldn't go on, working eighteen-hour days and running a home, looking after her children. While I sympathised, I had to say that there was no way in which we could alter the job to accommodate her. When I interview women, I ask if they are planning on having a family. Why not? A small firm like mine depends upon the availability of staff to serve our clients.

"It is not a question of my personal beliefs, but on how someone's commitment to the job, or lack of it, is going to affect everyone else."

Kean, a mother of two, says: "I was fortunate because at the time I first became pregnant, I had been a partner in my firm for five years, and my position affords me more flexibility than many other women in my profession, even though I work very long hours."

A few female lawyers are lucky enough to have husbands who work at home and can take over the primary responsibility of child care. But typically one junior barrister was told by her senior female colleagues: "Don't have children if you really want to get on." It is not unknown for a woman lawyer to have three nannies 'just in case' for a defendant cannot have his trial stopped midway because of his lawyer's family commitments.

The most fundamental problem women lawyers face is an inherently male career structure. To deviate from it usually means losing the ultimate prize – QC status or equity partnership. The reality is clear. There is no right time to have children and, even in the case of barristers who are technically self-employed, there is no alternative to working in chambers.

A female QC explains the dilemma: "If you take a career break in your thirties to have children it can really be damaging, because that's just when your career really starts to take off, when you start being noticed by judges. When you do come back, it's demoralising – you have to start doing all the junior work again. Having a family when you are

Media solicitor, Caroline Kean

Lawyers

trying to build up your practice is equally fraught and is compounded by the worry of having to support yourself for the first few years."

In this respect solicitors have it easier, since they earn a salary from the beginning and do not have to contend with such a male-dominated profession. "I have never had any firm say that they did not want women," says recruitment consultant David Woolfson. "These days you find women in all areas, even in such traditionally macho ones as construction law, or the heavyweight disciplines such as banking, capital markets, corporate finance and project finance. It is true that firms are still predominantly male at partner level, but that is changing."

In the US women are very highly represented within the ranks of associates (salaried lawyers), but their numbers drop off steeply at partnership level for exactly the same reasons as their British counterparts. California attorney Madelyn Chaber says: "It is particularly hard for women to break into the large law firms which represent the big conglomerates, and become defence attorneys. Traditionally, this has always been white-man's territory. There were efforts being made by many of those firms to recruit more women and elevate some to partnership level. But I don't know what affect proposition 209, the anti-affirmative action proposition, will have on this."

Chapter Three

MAKING AN ENTRANCE

"You get in, I'd say, if your face fits," says barrister Daphne Loebl. "People tend to select in their own image. They think, 'We want someone like us, because obviously that is what works.' It's a kind of survival device with which they mark their own territory and differentiate it from other practices. In each case selection is controlled by existing members of the group; hence the similarity to a club.

"There is an absence of stated or even identified selection criteria, or any effective procedure for applying those criteria to the selection process. It means you may be selected for qualities that are not central to the job definition: you happen to conform in style and type to the barristers already there, and so does your method of work. This explains how you get a white, male-dominated Bar and judiciary but, by the same token, it means that a woman, with the qualities a certain set feels to be essential, will be more likely to be admitted to it than a man without those qualities. It has been called a system of patronage, and it is."

Whilst Loebl is referring specifically to how barristers gain entry to practise law, her observation could apply to the legal profession as a whole. The fundamental problem for 'outsiders' is highlighted in the tightly knit world of the Bar in which chambers are very reluctant to accept any deviation from the traditional norm whether it be "white, male and middle-class" or first-class university degrees only. A male QC agrees that 'selecting the familiar' is the easier option. "But it doesn't in any way cut out someone with a first-class brain who doesn't share, say, an Oxbridge background; it just makes it easier for those who do." Or as one of his distinguished colleagues, who did not exactly fulfill his potential at university, says: "We would look sympathetically upon someone with a second-class degree from Exeter." The underlying principles apply to solicitors as well as barristers.

TIER SYSTEM

The distinction of one's set of chambers is, perhaps, the crucial factor, in determining individual success. Just like the British Football League there is a Premiership division followed by Divisions 1,2, and 3.

"There is also a Corinthian league," says one barrister with a shudder. Members of the Bar and their clerks will generally acknowledge that about 15% – 20% of the profession are first-rate, 5% are dire and the remainder, "average, run of the mill, steady, mediocre."

One ignores or is ignorant of the tier system at one's own peril. A successful practitioner of administrative law and judicial review recounts her own experience – a cautionary tale if ever there was one. "Everyone has to work hard to succeed, but I made it harder for myself than I need have. I completed a law degree as a mature student and then became a law lecturer, but I wasn't aware of the way the system worked. I wasn't Oxbridge, I previously taught in a polytechnic, and I wasn't impressed by names, not just because of my own background but because I knew that the reputations of some of the big names weren't justified.

"When I decided to practise, I didn't get in initially because of my age and sex, and I'm not sure how valid this is, because I wasn't in the first flight of academics. I have always assumed that had I taken a professorship before I came to the Bar I might have found it easier to have been accepted by a good set of chambers. My profile didn't fit, and the two or three chambers that specialise in the sort of work I do wouldn't have me. One or two sets admitted quite openly that they couldn't take me because I was older and had better connections – some of my former students had become solicitors – and I would do better than their present junior tenants who would regard me as unwelcome competition and so vote against taking me on.

"The chambers I actually went to did not consider this, which was unfortunate, because one of the precipitating factors in my dispute with the set was that I earned more than them. The irony is that I was told not to do legal aid work because 'we don't do that sort of thing, we do commercial work,' and that chambers' solicitors wouldn't instruct me if I worked for law centres. I replied that there was no reason for them to know but in the end I had only my legal aid work.

Lawyers

"I was so busy trying to establish myself and thinking they considered me a failure that I didn't notice what was actually happening. Then in 1994, chambers' earnings were published and it came out that I had billed more than anyone else, including those senior to me. In retrospect I can see that I was showing them up and considering how junior I was, they didn't like it."

This female barrister paid a heavy price for joining a chambers where she so obviously did not fit. She subsequently became engaged in a long-running and costly lawsuit with her former set; its members secretly resigned, saddling her with all the debts and liabilities of the defunct chambers. She, too, abandoned the old chambers and set up on her own when her present office in Lincoln's Inn became available. She was later joined by another female barrister from that set who had left shortly before her.

Michael Mansfield, on the other hand, may have a reputation for being a firebrand, rebel and radical defence QC, but his early training with two very establishment sets means he possesses the kind of impeccable pedigree the most conservative barrister would relish. Mansfield, like our previous example, possessed no legal connections, but he was lucky.

He asked the Treasurer at Middle Temple to help find a chambers willing to give him a pupillage. "I think he was shocked that somebody hadn't got an automatic route through his tie and socks straight into some set of chambers. I was probably regarded as some sort of legal vagrant." That very afternoon Mansfield was interviewed and accepted by a first-rate establishment set.

This placement and his next, at 5 Paper Buildings, home of the then Treasury Counsel (the Government's legal adviser), were extremely fortuitous, as they allowed the establishment to get to know Mansfield 'in fact' rather than by reputation.

"Those within the establishment who only knew my reputation thought I was a 'red under the bed'. Those who knew me in fact realised I could be trusted, had a certain competence and was all right so I wasn't therefore a loose cannon," says Mansfield.

Even when he left to establish his own chambers outside The Temple his personal credibility was never at issue but such a move was regarded then as an extremely risky and unusual move to make, and jokes were made that it would become the 'Kremlin on the hill'.

Today's trainee barristers have access to more information than in Mansfield's day through the pupillage guide books. A new clearing-house has been introduced where pupillage applications can be centrally processed but the highly competitive state of the Bar means that there is less likelihood of being taken on by a set if one's CV or profile is not a perfect fit.

As homogeneity increasingly rules, flamboyant initiatives 'a la Mansfield' have become depressingly rare. Now as then, the luck factor remains high. One barrister, asking about a set that listed his specialist field in The Bar Directory, was told, "Well, they might have done one of those cases about ten years ago."

Another aspirant, Jim Buchanan was warned off one

particular set: "Don't go there even if they pay you," said a friend already at the Bar, who had been asked by Buchanan to name the best 15 sets from a list of all the criminal chambers.

Buchanan is one of the new breed of barristers. The product of a non-legal, typically lower middle/working class family, he went to Nottingham University to study law in 1984. "I completed the first year but didn't like it. There was no criminal law. I had come from a comprehensive school and so there had been nobody to warn me how varied the syllabus can be from one university to another."

He completed a history degree instead and then traveled around the world for two years. He spent a further year in Asia as a tour guide to pay for the law conversion course and continued working in the travel industry here in the UK to earn the then £4000 fee required to sit the Bar Finals. His 12-month pupillage was unpaid but, unusually, he was taken on straight-away by a highly regarded specialist criminal set led by Jonathan Goldberg. "It's a fair mix of backgrounds and educations here. There is a barrister three years my senior who was the only student from his school at the time ever to have gone to university, so he has a very similar background to mine.

"There is no question in my mind that it makes things easier if you come from a traditional background, say public school and Oxford. Not simply because of the old-boy network but because, as in so many professions, they like to recruit from their own; it's the easy option. My impression, or prejudice, is that they like to look at a CV and know precisely what they are getting. For instance, my profile or CV would probably not have fitted the pukka, establishment prosecutor sets.

"I have got to where I am now because I am more motivated and work harder. I am told that I am motivated by a chip on my shoulder and I suspect this is true. It doesn't manifest itself in any unpleasant way, but I am driven."

Buchanan and his ilk, through sheer weight of numbers, are eroding the stereotype of the upper-middle-class barrister who depends on his wealthy family for support because, unlike the solicitor, he cannot count on an income while training and establishing a reputation.

There have, of course, always been barristers who have paid their own way, but they were rare. When John Jarvis, QC started out, he had to pay a pupillage fee of 100 guineas to his pupil master and his clerk (the former received the pounds, the latter the shillings) a scheme abolished in 1972.

While training, he worked evenings and weekends as a private tutor. "Having gone through it this way I

John Jarvis, QC

am not sympathetic to people saying how hard this career is. If you have to work in a pub to have this career, you do it."

For the past six years a recommended, minimum award amounting to £4,000 to £5,000 per annum has been in place although in some chambers that has led to a cutback in the numbers of pupils being taken on.

Barrister Quincy Whitaker says the profession at junior level is no longer dominated by those with public school backgrounds. "There are plenty of state educated people who are barristers – I went to a comprehensive. But it is much easier to get in if you are state school and Oxbridge educated, as I was, than if you are from a state school and poly(technic) background."

HUDDLING TOGETHER

One of the intrinsic advantages of an Oxbridge education is a cosy familiarity with the language, habitat and customs of the profession which can seem alien and arcane, if not downright absurd at times, to everybody else.

The four Inns of Court (barristers must register at one when they embark upon their careers) are virtually an extension of the college structures at Oxford and Cambridge. The buildings in which barristers huddle together in their sets are simply upgraded models of Kings' or St. John's students' rooms, or at senior level, reminiscent of a don's room. The terms when senior judges sit, are similar in length and name to those of Oxford; Hilary, Trinity, and Michaelmas. Indeed, according to one commercial QC, the atmosphere in court, with the exception of major criminal trials, should ideally feel like a debate in a don's room.

Inevitably, judicial ways of thinking are heavily influenced by Oxford and Cambridge – the alma maters of all but 17 of the 140 High Court judges. One solicitor, David Bigmore, recalls his student interview: "I was asked by the admissions tutor why I wanted to read law. I said, 'That's a leading question,' to which, he replied, 'No, it's not. A leading question is when a barrister is leading the witness in the course of his examination.' My tutor had been trained to think in such a way that he could not understand how anyone, even an 18-year-old in winkle-picker shoes and drainpipe trousers, could be unversed in what a leading question was. It had become second nature for him to view things from a very specific legal perspective."

As academic élitism increases its hold, the traditional public school background is correspondingly losing its influence. Traces of "public school redolence," says Mansfield, QC are nowadays mainly confined to the four Inns of Court: Inner Temple, Middle Temple, Gray's Inn and Lincoln's Inn. These Inns were established some time in the fourteenth century (early records have been lost) and are where Oliver Goldsmith wrote, Charles Dickens and his characters worked, and Shakespeare's company put on the first performances of some of his plays.

The sense of 'clubbiness' is at its most intense in the dining halls, where barristers consume their soup, meat and three veg., cheese and pie at long, narrow tables, beneath portraits of the founders. "It's like any works canteen, really," said one barrister, alluding to the halls' closeness to the chambers and courts, the cheap, quick meals and the company of colleagues. (The analogy somewhat falters when one considers the centuries-old paintings, the gilded cornices and the quality of the wine cellar).

To qualify as barristers, law students are obliged to eat 18 dinners a year at their chosen Inn, even if they are studying law hundreds of miles away. Students living abroad can eat their 18 dinners in three weeks. These dinners were originally introduced to give trainee barristers the opportunity to meet each other because the Bar course was done by correspondence. But the generally held view nowadays is that, once the Inns of Court School of Law was founded the dinners became a pointless ritual.

"Even though the dinners are subsidised, it's still an expense, although if you join an Inn as soon as you start university, at least you can spread the cost over three years. The idea is that you are supposed to meet and learn from those senior to you. In fact, you end up sitting with your friends who were with you at Bar school, eating school-dinner stodge," says Quincy Whitaker.

A committee member of an Inn admits: "Many young diners think their time here is a dead loss. They do the minimum to get through the evening. But he advises: "The sooner they realise that the dinners are really an extremely useful form of networking, the better. They can discover, before they seek pupillage, the best and worst sets in the areas in which they want to specialise."

Making an Entrance

The Inns provide more substantial help as well, offering a variety of scholarships available. Nonetheless, the younger generation of barristers tend to regard those who spend more than the required amount of time at the Inn, and even seem to enjoy it, as 'sadsters'.

"Dining is supposed to give you the social mores of the day and imbue you with the right social standards. It absolutely doesn't," says Mansfield. "It was anachronistic when I had to attend, and the behaviour and sexism at these dinners was appalling."

It still can be. A female barrister recalls dining one night at Gray's Inn, notorious for its eccentric customs and schooboyish ways, and being offered a large sum of money by a senior member of the Bar to streak round the inn. She walked out.

Although many women find the Bar's public school ambiance repellent, that 'clubbishness' makes it enormously attractive to some men. "I was taken by my father, who was a barrister, to lunch at Gray's Inn when I was ten," one QC recalled. "All the men behaved just the way we did at school but clearly had much more fun. They were laughing and throwing bread at one another. And I thought, 'This is marvelous. If I become a barrister, I can stay in this world for the rest of my life'."

Ferguson, QC, says the Bar has a lot besides bun-throwing in common with the English public school. "You start as a 'fag' at the bottom and work your way up to prefect, which is almost like being a QC or very experienced junior barrister – you are trusted and given special responsibilities. Then, finally, you become a judge, the equivalent of being a teacher, and look with favour upon those who were prefects with you, because of your shared background.

"A barrister may be thick but what matters is whether or not he's a 'good chap'.

"If the woman barrister wants to get along in her professional life, she has to be a chap as well, because public schoolboys who spend their formative years in isolation from women, feel uncomfortable with them and don't know how to cope with them on any other level."

Quincy Whitaker believes the Bar at its most junior is 'fairly representative' of society, except in terms of class. "Class will be the last thing to go at the Bar. I don't hear barristers with really strong regional or working-class accents, to speak in outdated terms."

Ferguson says that when he started out, he was told by a senior colleague that, no matter how brilliant a lawyer he might turn out to be, his accent would hinder him and advised him to drop it. He refused and time has proved him right. He finds his strong Ulster accent marks him out so that people, impressed with his performance, may ask for 'the Irishman'.

While regional accents from Scotland, Ireland and Wales may, in rare instances, be regarded as an interesting feature, English ones are not. Criminal QC, Alun Jones says: "I used to speak with a Liverpool accent. It wasn't that strong but it was recognisable. I didn't make any conscious effort to get rid of it but I was aware that Liverpool accents, like Birmingham or cockney accents, don't go down well at the Bar. You are expected to speak the Queen's English. After five years in London, I met an old girlfriend from university and she said, 'You've lost your accent'."

Nothing has changed; indeed, it may be worse. Mansfield knows of barristers who have taken elocution lessons and 'positively purified' themselves of their accents. The younger generation, in particular, are worried that it might prevent them from being taken on by a set of chambers. So it seems that TV's fictional character, Kavanagh, QC, is likely to remain the only prominent barrister with a distinct northern accent.

Alun Jones, QC, the grammar-school son of an insurance clerk from Liverpool, says: "I have many criticisms of the English legal system but I do not think it excludes anybody at all. My impression of the Bar is that it is a mixture of 20 – 30% barristers whose parents were lawyers, 30-40% who come from similar backgrounds such as the church or Foreign Office, and a good 30% who come from any background at all.

"It is one of the good things about the

Richard Ferguson, QC

Lawyers

Bar that there is no impediment to people like me joining, those with no connection at all with the law. On the
other hand, I do think people representing the government in prosecution cases and in judicial review
proceedings do tend to have a public school background.
But that's only a slight imbalance. Previously, in Lord
Hailsham's day, you would have had four criminal barristers made up to QC, three of them prosecutors. Now
people are selected much more on merit; there are a lot
more Jewish people, ethnic minorities and women, irrespective of background, who are QCs."

RACIAL PREJUDICE
The fact that there are a number of successful black
and Asian, as well as numerous Jewish, solicitors and
barristers, bears this out. It would be foolish, however, to
discount the existence and extent of prejudice in areas
where there has been no compelling motive for it to
disappear. Many of the non-traditional success stories
owe their existence to the increasing number and wealth
of non-white, non-Christian clients, often foreign ones.

As most lawyers admit, there is less discrimination
about than there used to be, but it has hardly disappeared. It can assume a very subtle form. A barrister
specialising in civil law says that, because he is black, an
assumption was made during job interviews that he
would become a criminal lawyer. "Civil law purports to
be more intellectually rigorous, and so I was not thought
to be an obvious candidate."

Usually, it is more obvious. An eminent non-Jewish

solicitor, whose partners are Jews, confesses he has been told that he is the 'acceptable face' of the firm. His main rivals are Jewish and because of this, the senior partner believes his firm does not have the same status.

The head of another Jewish firm says he has not bothered to apply for membership of certain golf and gentlemen's clubs because he knows he would not be accepted.

Another non-Jewish solicitor who previously worked in two predominantly Jewish firms agrees there is a degree of clannishness to be found in both Jewish and non-Jewish firms. "There was no difference in terms of practice. The difference lay with whom the firms did business. People want to do business with those with whom they feel at ease, and it's much easier to get on if you have a common factor.

"In my last firm, if you were a practising Jew, it probably helped. There was a lot of networking done in the Jewish community and, yes, I did feel a little excluded. The playing field was level, but there was more equality for some than others. Although my first firm was possibly more traditionally Jewish, it wasn't until the last three or four years in my second firm that I would hear things which made me aware that not everybody picked their firm of lawyers objectively."

According to this solicitor, it would appear that the attitudes underlying such clannishness are subtly different: There is a suspicion that when WASPS (white Anglo-Saxon Protestants) get together, it is based on a desire to feel superior and exclude, but when Jewish

Lawyers

people get together, they are simply not including you.

Some young lawyers have been asked by their employers or head of chambers if they would mind shortening or anglicising their names. It would, they are told, make things easier, and that does not just mean spelling. Other candidates whose applications have been rejected have applied again under another, more bland name and been granted an interview – some have then sued the firm for discrimination.

A few of these prosecutions succeed, but on the whole discrimination is very difficult to prove. Perhaps one could say that, right at the beginning of his career, such an aspirant is being confronted with the lawyer's perpetual choice between gaining his point and winning the game.

Chapter Four

RISING STARS

The 'nice guy' personality is the one most prized by solicitors, barristers and judges alike. For all the emphasis on intellectual ability, it is not enough.

"I remember one applicant, a Cambridge graduate, who had three firsts," says John Jarvis, QC. "He was obviously very clever, perfectly well turned out, but the opinion of everybody interviewing him was 'I do not like him.' He grated on people. You do not want that, because not only is that going to be unpleasant in chambers, but someone who irritates you is going to irritate the judge."

It is important to get on with other members of the firm or set but it becomes vital if one wishes to survive at partnership level. "Partnership," says one senior solicitor, "is a most unnatural relationship. It is much more intimate than marriage in a sense, because when you are made a partner you are not in a position to pick and choose who will be in the firm, and you find yourself beside people you did not or would not pick as full partners.

"It is a very bad way of doing business because everyone has an equal vote and, theoretically, every decision, down to the thickness of the notepaper, has to be sanctioned by the partners. Sometimes there is a majority vote and for the really big decisions, unanimity is required, which is stultifying - desperately so."

SELLING SKILLS

Conflicts amongst lawyers working in such close proximity are inevitable, but ultimately partners have to defer to their common goals. Those who sow dissension will not uncommonly find themselves ousted from the firm.

Recruitment consultant David Woolfson says that, since the recession in the early 1990's, 'client development' skills have assumed even greater importance. "You will find that the solicitors who are made up to partner, and this is across the board, are those who are good at either attracting or retaining major clients. Lawyers are operating in a market which is much more competitive than it used to be, so firms want people who can sell, and who can persuade potential clients to use their firm rather than the one down the road.

An up-and-coming commercial solicitor confirms this. "It is essential to be able to relate to the person who is hiring you. In the insurance market, for instance, you are dealing with guys who don't have any formal education. They get into the markets at an early age, seventeen or eighteen, as a runner, become underwriters or brokers, and move up the hierarchy. Now, my boss went to Oxford, he is a very cultivated man, but he can appeal to people whose idea of a good time is spending the evening drinking a lot. He knows how to talk to them, how to maintain a relationship with them."

This ability can not only attract and keep business but can save the lawyer's neck when he has made an expensive mistake. "If you overlook the one document that would have proved your case, that can be forgotten if your client chooses to say 'No problem', and forgives you."

Little wonder then, that 'shmoozing' with clients is an integral part of a solicitor's life. Membership in a club such as the Athenaeum, the RAC or the Reform is an advertisement of one's success and 'clubbability' as well as a strong card in the consumer-relations game. "There is nothing our American clients like more," says one solicitor, "than being taken to a Pall Mall club."

BEING SEEN

Profitable socialising increasingly goes on in more casual contexts. "It used to be frowned on for members of the Bar to be seen in places that were less than strait-laced. Not anymore," says a senior in-house solicitor. "I go around Soho and see lawyers propping up the bar at 2 a.m., as well they should. You have got to go where your clients go, and where you can talk to all sorts of people. If I am going to get people half my age on a jury, then I have got to know what makes them tick."

Lawyers with a lack of legal ability have been known to make a living on the strength of personality. In two separate instances, when solicitors were asked why they kept giving work to an incompetent barrister, they replied, "He gets on well with the clients." An in-house lawyer who was told this says: "It's absolutely the worst reason. It also arises because solicitors' firms have pet sets; that is, when they have work they give it to one particular set of chambers, not because the barrister there is necessarily an expert, but because they get on well with him and he has dealt with a number of matters for them in the past."

He cited as an example a firm of solicitors which represented a bank, where he worked as an in-house lawyer, that always sought advice from the same barrister. "It was a standing joke between my line manager at the bank and me that this barrister could be an expert in all those different fields. It was impossible. But the solicitors had a good rapport with that barrister. As John Mortimer said once, 'They liked the cut of his jib.'"

Nowadays, because of the complexity of business deals, it is common for commercial solicitors to be on secondment at city firms for up to three years and, yes, says one merchant banker, personality plays a crucial role. "Sometimes I am working with lawyers in the same office until 2a.m, and it's absolutely essential we get on because I must have confidence in what they tell me. I can only have that confidence if they communicate clearly what I need to know – and ease of communication has to do with a good personality."

One law firm asks candidates to explain their approach to a problem to one of its secretaries, who afterwards reports on whether they have been clear but not condescending. Media solicitor, Caroline Kean makes a point of asking applicants a legal question during recruitment interviews, designed to test their knowledge and ability to communicate. "I look for approachability in the people I pick. In my work I may be dealing with a company rather than an individual, but the company is made up of individuals.

"What makes people valuable to me, whether they are solicitors or barristers, is that, if you ask them questions, they do not simply give you a dissertation on the law or tell you the pros and cons and say that you have to decide. Instead, they show how the law applies to this particular case, and then, on that basis, give their advice on what should be done. I feel my job is to say to clients, 'This is the best thing you can do, based on my experience.' I am paid to stick my neck out."

She is well aware, however, of a feeling amongst the public that lawyers are generally a waste of time and money. "What's more, I think it is true. 20% of the profession as a whole subscribe to what I call 'good practice', and the rest do not. "When I studied law it was a bit of a shock to realise that, out of the 40 people in my class, there were only three I actually would have wanted to represent me. It dawned on me that this percentage was probably true of all the classes across all the law colleges in my year – it was very disappointing."

POOR PERFORMANCE

Some of these, of course, qualify as solicitors and are counted in the statistics, but do not actually practise. Throughout the UK there are, according to 1995 -1996 figures, approximately 94,817 solicitors qualified to practise,18, 676 of whom do not. Nonetheless, genuine dismay

Lawyers

is expressed by top lawyers at the mediocre performance of many of the 76,141 who do.

'Milking a client' is a major cause of concern. "A lawyer's fees are worked out according to the hours he takes to do a particular job. It seems curious," says one senior commercial solicitor, "that if you spend a long time on a case, you are paid more than if you cut through to the heart of the matter and expedite it quickly." In the US, the same problem exists. Attorney Madelyn Chaber says: "If you are on the side that bills by the hour I wouldn't say that the quickness incentive is necessarily there."

Another says: "When I talk about lawyers 'milking the system', I don't mean that they cynically set about running a case for as long as possible. But they certainly do keep taking steps in an action without necessarily thinking about where they are going." The consequences for the client when lawyers lose sight of the objective are appalling and expensive, he adds.

IDLENESS

Penny Darbyshire, Senior Law Lecturer at Kingston University, who has spent the past three summers observing the court system in action, from magistrates' courts to the House of Lords, says: "One of the shocking findings was the lack of competence in criminal advocacy at every level. Throughout, there was an obvious lack of preparation, inadequate advocacy skills and ignorance of the law. The poor service in the county courts and magistrates' courts is partly due to lack of money, but it is also partly caused by lawyers' idleness."

One leading commercial QC confided that, while acting as a part-time recorder in Knightsbridge Crown Court, he had been horrified at the incompetence of a criminal barrister appearing before him. "I have no idea why solicitors continue to use him. The only recourse I have is to report him to his chambers and they probably know how inadequate he is. I am ashamed he shares my profession."

SECOND OPINION

Negligent advice is also regarded as an ugly symptom of mediocrity within the profession. One senior barrister tells of a firm of solicitors who advised their client, a professional nanny, to accept £1,500 compensation after she suffered a whiplash injury in a car accident and was unable to work for many months.

"She came to see me and I told her to reject it. The insurance company immediately upped its offer to £3,000. I insisted that a figure of around £7,500 to £10,000 was more appropriate and had someone write a second opinion to confirm this. If this nanny hadn't known me, she would have been fobbed off with a very low settlement. It is worrying to think how many other people have been in the same situation. I am sure it's just the tip of the iceberg."

For the sad truth is that the average citizen is pretty clueless about where he stands legally and has only the vaguest notion of what he hopes to achieve through legal action. If someone slips on a paving stone, he is nine out of ten times more likely to ask the solicitor what to do than to have any clear objective, such as suggesting that

Lawyers

the local council compensate him.

It is no wonder then, that the public at large feels so vulnerable dealing with lawyers, particularly, as one senior solicitor remarks: "Most people are so profoundly ignorant of the law and what they can expect from it, that they are not even in a position to distinguish between a good and a bad lawyer." Penny Darbyshire feels to strongly about the level of service that she says: "I am just thankful that I am a lawyer, therefore, I do not have to rely on other lawyers."

RIGHTS AND REDRESS

Personal injury barrister Jacqueline Perry, who under the pseudonym Nicola Charles was a legal broadcaster on the Jimmy Young radio show and the 'Richard and Judy' morning television programme, believes strongly that all too often a fear of legal costs and general ignorance about the law mean that many people are left to put up with intolerable or unhappy situations: "There is a growing public awareness of entitlement to 'rights' and 'redress,' but most people do not know where to look or whom to ask when things go wrong." Perry is in no doubt

---

* Know Your Law' by Nicola Charles and Janice James addresses the legal problems which concern the public most. They include divorce, job sackings, children's schools and related problems, neighbours, noise and nuisance, live-in lovers and their rights, and medical matters such as suing your doctor. It also advises when to seek professional advice and when it would be wasting time and money.

that the public wants to know more.

Some 1500 people used to phone in with their legal questions during her TV appearances which prompted her to co-write a question and answer general legal guide*. She would also like to see a basic legal course as part of the school curriculum.

"We will not be creating a nation of lawyers but simply giving our young people an insight into fundamental legal principles so that they can have some idea where they stand in the community as consumers of goods and services and what is expected of them as citizens, parents and neighbours. It will enable them to acquire a basic understanding of the way the legal process works."

Equally, they would be able to better identify the good lawyers, and avoid the bad ones, as well as know what standard of service they should be able to expect.

The public perception of the client as lawyer's pawn was encapsulated in a strip cartoon featuring two lawyers. One said he would not be at Ascot because he had a case about to go to trial, but the other insisted that there must be some way of extricating himself. In the next frame the lawyer was shown talking to his client. He advised him that he would lose and that a plea bargain was in order. The cartoon ends with the two lawyers at Ascot.

A leading QC observes: "My contemporaries, a huge number of whom are in their middle to late 40's, have become jaded and settled for a certain lifestyle. They don't want to work too hard: they just want to chug along, have lots of holidays - they no longer have ambition. Yet

Lawyers

those who think of themselves, to some extent, as outsiders seem to maintain their enthusiasm a lot longer. Very few of them have settled in the way I have described."

An ambitious junior barrister explains that, while it is acceptable, indeed necessary, to sacrifice one's personal life when building a practice, values and priorities can alter when a spouse and family enter the frame: "A pile of papers can be dumped on my desk at 6pm which means my working until 2am, and then I am off to court early next morning. Or else, papers arrive on Friday night and my weekend arrangements have to be cancelled. That's fine now, because my profession is the most important factor in my life, but whether in a few years time that will still be true, I'm not sure. I don't think it is healthy or acceptable to be in a situation where you see your wife briefly in the mornings and evenings, and your children grow up virtual strangers. You have to try and strike a balance between being a professional and personal success."

The ascent of the ambitious solicitor and barrister share certain similarities. Both know the value of a 'make-you' case and hope fervently it will come their way, as it did for solicitor Stephen Pollard, who acted for Nick Leeson in the Barings Bank collapse, or for barrister Clare Montgomery, who worked on the Kevin Maxwell case and was subsequently made QC. There is a negative aspect, however. Sean Gates, an aviation solicitor, was catapulted into pre-eminence when he was asked to handle the claims which arose from the 1983 Korean air disaster, in which an airliner was shot down. "I was 34, and this was the biggest case in aviation history. It was a huge high but the problem for me was that it came too soon in my career. Now I face a lot more of the same type of work but no new challenges."

Youth is regarded as an advantage by virtually all leading law firms and sets, and priority is given to university graduates who are easier to mould into their own image. Bucking the trend is by no means impossible, though, if one is exceptional. One former trade union representative-turned-barrister spectacularly make QC within five years of practice; it usually takes anywhere between 15 and 18 years to achieve this status.

Experience may be an advantage if it is relevant. "Two years in a bank or insurance company does give you a practical background," says John Jarvis, QC.

PEER GROUPS

Above all, the essential quality is fitting in. "At this stage in my career, I am trying to establish myself as the 'good, old, new boy'," says one ambitious solicitor. "I am a protected son for two reasons. I trained with this firm, and there is always going to be a difference between someone who comes in and has not been brought up in the firm's culture, and someone who is in-house.

"Also, I am the only one in my peer group who has brought in clients. What I generate is allocated to one of the equity partners, which increases his share of the pie. I do not benefit directly yet, but one day my boss will turn over a meeting and then a client to me."

Lawyers

In some firms, the elevation to partner is a process clearly laid out, with solicitors knowing where they are in the hierarchy or lock step, as it is technically called. They collect points for each year with the firm and according to the number of points they have accrued, move upwards to the next level where they will all be paid a set amount. If they continue to be successful, they will progress along what is described as a slowly-moving escalator to the very top, known as the plateau, to become equity partners.

Once a sinecure for life, remaining in a partnerships has to be earned every year. Law firms now commonly conduct an annual cull, on the theory that, as one lawyer put it, "if you don't lose the bad ones this year, you'll lose the good ones next year."

Nonetheless, on the ascent, it still does not do to be obviously better than some of the existing partners, as that can be a great source of animosity and in some instances prevent full partnership. "Being one of the guys is the best way to disarm those who may feel threatened – and get ahead," observes a young solicitor.

The same applies at the Bar, where there is a tendency for nice guys to be made QCs before the others. Alun

---

* The gown is unlikely to be 100% silk since they cost more than £1,000, twice the price of a silk blend and four times the cost of a polyester type. Most barristers rent or borrow a real silk for the QC ceremony. Cherie Booth, Prime Minister's wife, borrowed both wig and gown from her head of chambers, Lord Irvine, now Lord Chancellor.

Jones, QC says: "If you have the choice between a chap who is liked and average, and a chap who is bright but unpopular because he is not one of the boys, the former will get silk earlier in his career than the latter." The key to being one of the boys, he says, is in, "not making enemies." "I have a theory that a lot of people do well at the Bar, as in many other areas of life, by keeping quiet. They develop a reputation for being deep because they do not commit themselves to an opinion immediately. I think people who are regarded as a little too pushy or ambitious are pushed back a bit."

HIGHER STATUS

Becoming a Queen's Counsel, or taking silk, so-called because one has the right to represent the crown, and to do so wearing a silken gown*, is the path to higher earnings and status. As barrister Daphne Loebl says: "It is the only promotion we get in our career at the Bar. If you don't get silk you are obliged to hand over all the time to somebody who has. They get the glory and are, in fact, making the decisions and calling the shots while you are there to service them.

Michael Mansfield, who is against the two-tier system in principle, took silk after pressure from his set who felt that a head of chambers should be a QC – and because not being a QC would have prevented him from leading the defence cases in which he was interested. "A movement began, which is still going on to cleanse the profession of juniors who were regarded as somewhat unacceptable. The way to do this was to ensure that certain cases, particularly legal aid cases, required a silk."

Lawyers may apply to the Lord Chancellor's office each November to become a QC. In an effort to be seen as open and above board, the department sends out a detailed form with accompanying guide-lines which the silk applicant has to complete. No such guide-lines are deemed necessary for the selectors and, certainly, no written explanations of their choices are required, although they can, if they wish, volunteer reasons.

BEHIND CLOSED DOORS

If unsuccessful, the candidate can apply to find out why – in theory at least. One rejected silk applicant says: "The promotion process is not really any more open than it was. When the Lord Chancellor's department says, 'Come along and talk to us,' all you hear are these guarded comments from anonymous sources, such as A thinks you are red hot but B has said you are absolutely a no-hoper. When you ask why B holds this opinion, they say, 'We can't tell you that.' Well, B may not like me, and how can I deal with B's comments unless I know the full circumstances of his reasoning?

"When you suggest that the discrepancy between A and B should be investigated, the department will say, 'Yes, we do need to find the reasons'. But, we the applicants, unlike the department, are not told what the reasons are and what's more, we are not meant to be told. The department, of course, keeps all the data manually, otherwise we would have access to it through the Data Protection Act, wouldn't we?"

Rising Stars

The result, says Mike Mansfield, QC is a frustrating series of clues and half clues, suggestions and observations that a barrister can do nothing about. "The canvassing is exterior gloss; it's the unspoken word, almost, which rules – and every year we continue to hear of people who should have got it but didn't because some judge or other senior person has blocked it."

Barrister, Jacqueline Perry, says that the Lord Chancellor's department may sincerely believe that silks are chosen on merit, but she asks: "How can they be? Consider the selection process. They ask a list of people, 'What do you think of this chap?' and this chap happens to come from the same chambers they did, or is known to them personally or by family connections.

"They are bound to be more favourable to someone they know. In every walk of life there is nepotism. We all practise it. I will favour a pupil of mine over and above somebody else's. I'm not blaming anybody. I'm just facing up to the way the system works."

Lawyers, who are in the 'right' sets and whose practice and

Barrister, Jacqueline Perry

reputation are sufficiently advanced, are often encouraged to apply. "Sometimes," says High Court judge Mr.
Justice Bell, "a senior judge who has been impressed by
a barrister's performance may ask whether he has
thought of applying for silk, or a senior member of your
chambers might says it's about time you had a go.

"If you are in a friendly chambers, someone junior to
you might say, 'I'd like to apply. Why don't you have a
crack before me'. In less friendly chambers, you might
hear that someone junior to you is planning to apply next
year and think, 'Well, I'm not going to let him get in first,
so I will apply this year'."

Soundings are taken by circuit judge leaders from
chairmen of Bar Associations, the London judges, and
High Court judges. So barristers making frequent court
appearances before the 'right' judges are at a considerable advantage over those who appear before deputy
judges, or largely in consultation.

An experienced personal injury lawyer complains that
eight out of ten of his cases, categorised as fit for hearing
by a High Court judge, are heard by deputies. "Even if you
have £1 million cases which involve silks and a fantastic
workload, it is no good if you are not seen by the right
people."

Some opinions count more than others according to
another female barrister: "Obviously, the higher-placed
ones, those in the club already, like a Court of Appeal or
High Court judge, carries more weight than the chairman
of your Bar Association. Bound to." For this very reason,
the decision in January this year by the Master of the

Rising Stars

Rolls, Lord Woolf to employ six judicial assistants to the Court of Appeal will, no doubt, become coveted appointments.

According to Christopher Clarke, QC, Chairman of the Legal Services Committee, the aim is to recruit, 'the brightest and best' pupils from the civil Bar. They might earn only £58.71 a day clearing the Court of Appeal's backlog but, as Clarke points out, what a golden opportunity this part-time, three-month stint represents for younger members of the Bar. Signing off with a flourish, he writes: "Lord Woolf wishes to make a spell as judicial assistant... a prestigious appointment."

A constant refrain is that those without set or social connections must be prepared to, 'network, network, network'. "Careers, I am sure," says Mansfield, QC, "can be helped greatly by a golf ball in the right hole."

There are radical barristers who have been known to cross into establishment territory in order to become serious QC contenders, such as the radical lawyer who made it his task to wine, dine and be seen at the Garrick and the Carlton clubs, the favourite haunts of judges. In his case, it worked. Radical barristers are more likely, though, to gain QC status because "it is better to have them on the inside, spitting out, than on the outside, spitting in," says one plain-speaking barrister.

Certainly, damning exposés, such as 'Eve was Framed', by Helena Kennedy, QC, about the problems women have with the law, or 'Presumed Guilty' by Mike Mansfield, detailing miscarriages of justice, lend credence to this view. Such books are also 'very sexy' in media terms and help get their authors known.

US divorce lawyer Marvin Mitchelson, who pioneered 'palimony' cases, credits much of his success within the Hollywood set to his rapport with the world's press. He freely admits that newsworthiness is one of the criteria that influences him when deciding whether or not to take on a case. "Most cases need a news hook, and I have become adept at knowing where to hang the hook."

Mitchelson has always gone in where angels, and certainly lawyers, feared to tread in pursuit of a meaty legal challenge and international headlines. He recalls for example the Rock Hudson/Mark Christian case: "I know Hollywood was offended because I was suing a movie idol's estate on the grounds his former lover may contract AIDS. The point is, I saw an important law in this."

MEDIA SKILLS

Knowing what will attract and what will repel potential clients, the public and colleagues has always been one of Mitchelson's great gifts – for media attention can, of course, in the US as well as Britain, contradict the adage that there is no such thing as bad publicity.

"It is important to get on with the media," says a solicitor, "but if you become known as a rent-a-quote, or have a reputation for your cases making the headlines, clients who wish to maintain low profiles will not come to you, and judges and other lawyers will lose respect for you."

Nonetheless it is accepted, even at the Bar, that publicity helps. "The demand for QCs in general," says one, "will never exceed supply. There is no day when you can't walk into the Inn and find a dozen QCs with nothing to do. What happens is that the purchasers are influenced by fashion and want names they have heard of – it is like buying Louis Vuitton luggage. They will pay enormous sums to be represented by somebody they have heard of, as opposed to somebody who, they are told, is just as good but is unknown to them."

CLERKS

Barristers were precluded from advertising until the 1990's and any marketing which existed was carried out by their clerks. An intermediary between barrister and solicitor, the clerk organises cases, arranges court dates and traditionally protects his master or mistress from any discussion of fees. "We are their agents," says one.

"There is a strictly held taboo," says solicitor Sean Gates, "on discussing money with your barrister. But, judging from the insights I have gained, it is absolute nonsense that the clerk doesn't, as soon as he has talked to the solicitor, say to the barrister, 'This is what they are proposing. What do you think?' It is the barrister's decision. New barristers, however, would be more dependent on the advice of the clerk as to what they should charge in order to keep work flowing into the set."

They also depend upon their clerk for their initial cases. "Should a barrister fall foul of his clerk at the start of his career, the clerks could easily say to a solicitor that he is not available, so in that sense, they could make or break his career," says Jarvis, QC. "But it is not in their

Lawyers

long-term interest to do so, as clerks' earnings are dependent on the work they gain for barristers."

These used to be a straight percentage of the barristers' fees (10% in the old days) but a more sophisticated structure: salary plus bonus or commission has gained favour in most sets. "Roughly speaking," says one clerk," the more established the set and the longer the clerk has been there, the more likely he is to be on a straight percentage." This can, in rare cases, amount to a six-figure annual income, more than is earned by some barristers.

Some chambers even ask the clerk which prospective pupils to accept, a measure that others deride as letting the tail wag the dog. "Clerks pretend to be subservient, in one set they even call me 'marm,' but in reality, they have the whip hand, the power to totally screw up your career," says one barrister. Another lawyer says he left the Bar and joined the Criminal Prosecution Service because he could not stomach the clerks' treatment of him, against which he was powerless. So it comes as no surprise when a newly-qualified barrister says: "While we don't exactly make tea for them, if they are busy and want us to lend a hand, we would be foolish not to do it."

In top chambers, some clerks will even recommend a barrister in another set, instead of one of their own, if the solicitor's first choice is not free. It is done on the basis that, if he passes a solicitor on to a first-rate lawyer in another set rather than an adequate one in his own, the grateful solicitor will put a lot more business his way. To say it goes against the grain, however, is putting it mildly.

"Barristers are by nature egocentric," says one establishment clerk, citing the case of a QC who introduced a solicitor to his set and was later furious when the solicitor was referred to one of his colleagues. "The solicitor wanted advice from a barrister who had recently dealt with a Parliamentary bill and we had just the person. But this other barrister ranted and raved, 'My case, my client, why am I not doing it?' Barristers are all prima donnas and can be very pompous, but the men are much worse than the women. The women are more sensible. They realise they can't do everything and that they are not the only ones who have to make a living in the set."

CONTROL

One leading QC speaks for many of his colleagues when he says: "I think all the clerks have too much control; they regard themselves as the people who really run the set, whereas they should be the servants. But that's our fault. The system is one of long-standing, and it is tolerated because we are all paid well, we get along and, on the whole, it works. But if we fell upon hard times, we would have to impose much stricter conditions on clerks, on their powers as well as their incomes."

A long-time clerk begs to differ. "There are barristers who think we are second-hand car dealers who are trying to get as much money for ourselves as possible. We are more like football managers. There has been many a clerk forced out because he was perceived as earning too much money, even though he was responsible for bringing in a big chunk of fee earning business."

Lawyers

However uneasily, barristers and clerks keep each other in check, one cannot help wondering that providence must surely have had a hand in placing these two extremes in such close proximity.

Clerks, collectively, are disparaged by solicitors, too. The main bone of contention has to do with barristers' court appearances, which clerks may have to book as much as a year ahead, a tricky business since the case may end up not going to trial.

The clerks protect the barristers by double and even triple-booking. This results in understandable anger from solicitors told a few weeks before a trial date that the barrister they have been counting on for a year is otherwise engaged. Clerk Michael Kaplan says: "We will accept a second case if we feel that the first case will be sorted out by then, but we do it with our barristers' consent. They agree with what we do until it goes wrong, then it is our fault. But in this day and age we have to take the chance. Clerks are the middlemen although it often feels like we are piggy-in-the-middle. You need pretty broad shoulders to handle the flak."

They are also well versed in excuses. "We have all had to cover for barristers who haven't completed work when they said they would, and are out at a three or four hour lunch when the exasperated solicitor calls," says another clerk.

Senior clerks have lunch every Friday and pool their gossip, making it well nigh impossible for solicitors to undercut them, for they know what the others charge and raise their fees in concert. If a firm of solicitors insist upon a barrister whom the clerk feels is "too experienced" for the case, he will sometimes ask a 'silly fee' to deter them. As one clerk says: "If they still want to go ahead, our response is, 'OK, but it's going to cost you'."

Conversely, a barrister who does not readily attract work will not find it easy to switch sets. Before taking on a new member, a set always asks its clerks what they know or can find out about him.

MANAGERS

Recently, some chambers have been hiring practice managers, who energetically market the set and encourage communication and criticism from solicitors, thus encroaching on the clerks' traditional area of authority. However, the old, perhaps archaic practice of clerkship with jobs held since boyhood, or even inherited from a father or uncle, is too well entrenched to be easily dug out.

Michael Kaplan's career is typical. At the age of 16, through the connections of his aunt, a legal executive, he started off as a bag carrier, trolley pusher, tea maker and general dogsbody. This still applies to junior clerks today, but a two-year college course now exists for them which they attend one afternoon a week. One set of chambers, however, upset the status quo recently by advertising for junior clerks whose qualifications were to include two 'A' levels.

To move up, a clerk accepts he has to move out, although there are still an exceptional few whose careers span some 41 years – from 15-year-old tea boy to senior

Lawyers

clerk – within the same chambers. Kaplan has moved
three times, and for 15 out of his 20 years as a clerk he
was instructed to address his barristers by their formal
titles. Then he joined 4-5 Gray's Inn Square, where everyone is on first name terms. It happens to be the set where
Cherie Booth, QC, works. So, in one of life's small ironies,
he now calls the Prime Minister's wife by her Christian
name.

Chapter Five

TOPPING THE BILL

Today, money is the main measure of success in professional life and within the legal species, City lawyers are at the top. They are in the business of making money and in the UK they congregate in London, regarded as the world capital of international law.

The 'big five' legal firms are involved in global commercial transactions that run into many billions of pounds in the heavyweight disciplines of banking, capital markets and corporate and project finance. Senior partners admit to earning £500,000 a year, but some who are on 'super equity' are known to earn double this and more. Middling partners in such firms and good, experienced city lawyers in more modest private practices will expect to make anywhere between £300,000 and £400,000 a year.

"Top commercial silks can earn a vast fortune, too," says solicitor David Bigmore, a leading specialist in franchising. "In really large, long-running cases, a 'star' QC can earn upwards of a million pounds."

"The size of business deals has gone up to such an extent that we are talking almost unimaginable sums," says Robert Lindsay, City Editor of The Lawyer. "Lawyers are not generating this, but they are reacting to the market or 'parasitising' it, as some in the City would say. There are so many lawyers working on these very big deals that the bankers often refer to them as parasites.

"It's not just the companies involved in the take-over or merger that need lawyers. The bank or, more usually, the syndicate of banks which wants to finance the acquisition needs a lawyer and so do the underwriters. On such a deal there could be 30 lawyers, 12 of them partners."

£15.8 BILLION

The 'usual suspects' head the league table from 'Acquisitions', a monthly magazine which shows the top ten legal advisors to companies in UK public takeovers by deal-value in 1996.

Linklaters & Paines, regarded as the Rolls Royce of City law firms, is ranked No.1 having advised on 12 deals with a total value of £15,890 million. Allen & Overy, is in second place, with 11 deals valued at £8,572 million, while Slaughter and May, and Freshfields take third and fourth positions, and Clifford Chance manages ninth place.

Undoubtedly, M & A (mergers and acquisitions), is one of the most financially rewarding specialisations for a City lawyer. One of the two biggest deals in 1996 was the four-way merger of Mercury, Bell Cablemedia, Nynex and Videotron, valued at about £5 billion. The Allen & Overy team of lawyers which advised Cable and Wireless in connection with the deal was headed by 7 partners. Even more were involved in the £1.4 billion merger between the newspaper and magazine group, United News and

Topping the Bill

Media plc and MAI – a total of 12 partners and 17 assistants.

One senior insider says: "In these 'big-five' law firms, Oxbridge firsts and upper seconds dominate, because the people they do business with are also from Oxford and Cambridge, and they prefer to work with people they know. So certain blue-chip companies will work only with certain law firms and, they in turn, will work only with certain élite commercial chambers or a specific silk."

This is changing rapidly at junior level, however, where one young lawyer says his intake of four years ago comprised many graduates from state comprehensives and universities, including red-brick and the Open University, from all over Britain. "I know our firm turned down people whose parents were judges or had connections in the City. At our level, we don't have the clout to bring in clients, so connections don't come into it. We were recruited for our potential."

"It's a team game, particularly in the large firms," says recruitment consultant

Franchise solicitor, David Bigmore

Lawyers

David Woolfson. "So if you are gregarious, run the London marathon, play cricket, it won't do you any harm. It mirrors the actual work of a lawyer in many ways: you have team game transactions in which everybody has to perform their function to the required standard or the whole process clogs up. " It is hardly surprising then, that the one name to cause a ripple of excitement in the City was that of rugby player Brian Moore, the former England hooker who joined a top commercial firm of solicitors in London as a personal injury lawyer.

The lawyer's main purpose is to help expedite a deal in 24 hours, 48 hours or " yesterday" anywhere in the world deemed fit by his client, whilst ensuring that his interests are protected. "If someone wants a £100 million deal done in a week or three days, then lawyers work 40-hour days and thankfully, nobody questions where the other 16 hours come from. This is what businesses are going to have to pay. An hourly City rate can be anything from £280 up to £450 for the top guy," says one high-flier.

US THREAT

American law firms such as Millbank, Tweed, Hadley and McLoy, or Sidley and Austin, however, pose a real threat to existing City law practices. They have either opened or expanded offices in London, and begun to recruit British solicitors so they can offer their multi-national clients advice under English or US law. Woolfson says: "We have been approached by some American law firms who have not gone public yet and want to keep a low profile. They know that if they can offer English and

New York law capability, they potentially have the edge over firms which can offer only one or the other."

Lawyers like most professionals in the City benefited from the boom in the late 1970's and 1980's. "Money became easier and freer to make. There was a real taste for it, and when people were making so much they didn't tend to question or criticise how much they were spending," says a City lawyer.

"The 1980's saw mergers and acquisitions in the US and London beyond anything anyone had previously imagined. Today the stakes are still higher - and the higher the risks, the more security our corporate clients want. It's a curious concept." The result, he says, is that impossible guarantees are demanded of lawyers, one of whose main functions is to take the blame if the deal falls through. "We, along with accountants, are there to be the scapegoats. And that's why I don't have a problem in the world charging high rates for what I do and for what the law does in general."

BAD ADVICE

This may be why in the US, and latterly in Britain, commerce and industry have developed a litigious streak: they are increasingly suing law and accountancy firms for bad advice. And it also explains why the first three or four pages of a lawyer's letter to his client are so often disclaimers. Companies are willing to pay for such qualified advice because, says a commercial solicitor: "If the transaction goes wrong or the company bid fails, the president of the company doesn't want to be left holding

Lawyers

the bag. He wants to have recourse to somebody else. It is to an extent, a re-allocation of corporate responsibility to the legal profession."

A financier at one of the City's leading merchant banks agrees to a certain extent. "The UK has become much more litigious and everybody's insurance policies are getting higher. This applies to lawyers, bankers and accountants. Nobody wants to take all the risks, so we seek specialist advice for ourselves and our clients in order that everything possible is done to protect our bank and our clients' interests. For instance, we would advise a client who wants to buy shares and is worried about the possibility of inside information, to talk to a lawyer to ensure everything is above board. It is not a case of trying to pass the buck to the legal or accountancy professions."

Whilst the City is currently experiencing a mini-boom, the recession which hit it in 1991 and 1992 took many legal firms by surprise, including at least two of the big five firms. Clifford Chance and Freshfields moved into new sumptuous offices shortly before the property market crashed and says one insider: "Their equity partners, who paid for the move, took a huge drop in earnings" during those years, adding: "It was more luck than judgment that other firms didn't follow suit and upgrade offices."

The long-term impact of the recession is that client companies, corporations, banks and industries have grown ever more cost-conscious. "Lawyers," says Lindsay, "unlike bankers are not allowed to take a percentage. In the old days, law firms in general would bill on an hourly basis; 50 hours at £300 an hour per lawyer was not unreasonable. Nowadays, it has become so competitive that firms have to put together an attractive package. Some will work for fixed fees with an element of performance thrown in: that's to say, if there's a hostile takeover, they will receive 100% of the fees only if the deal goes through."

So, to win new business and to retain existing clients, firms have had, on occasion, to bid low, even to the extent of charging uneconomic fees ('low-balling'). "The present climate is rather more favourable, but beauty parades (presentations by law firms to a potential client) and fee negotiations seem to be here to stay," says a report in the Chambers & Partners Recruitment Directory.

Though the big five don't actually use the word 'discount' they are prepared to be flexible to accommodate a major client. "A merchant bank like ours is regarded as a big client by the several law firms and specific lawyers within those firms whom we use," says a banker. "It is the client who calls the shots and so the lawyers know they have to take good care of us.

"We routinely shop around to find out who is available for a particular transaction and we agree a fee on each one. But if we feel there isn't enough legal work to warrant it, or we are not happy with the work, or say, the transaction fails, then we have subtle conversations re-negotiating price. We don't actually have to say, 'No we won't pay'. Naturally, we can't pay a success fee up front, but it is not uncommon to pay such a fee once the transaction is successfully completed."

Lawyers at the big five do not, as a rule, tell their clients what their hourly rates are – their log is for their own personal records, says an insider. "Fees vary from transaction to transaction, and during a transaction the client will be informed of any changes. Sometimes, the process takes longer because extra documents need to be drafted or extra issues come up. At the end, a lawyer will generally sit down with the client and discuss the fee. I have never seen a bill sent out without it being talked through with the client first."

One eminent City lawyer confirms that agreeing on price upfront is one of the few changes which has affected his 26-year long career: "I'm jealous of firms which don't have to agree to fixed price work. I can't be like that. Typically, what happens is that a customer wants something financed by a bank for whom we are acting. The bank tells the customer how much that will be and mentions the added fee for 'the legals' which is the cost of the legal work entailed.

"We resist it strongly if the customer asks for the legals to be capped because we can't tell how long the work is going to take. But I have a couple of Japanese banks for clients who occasionally say to me that they are not able to charge 'the legals' to the customer and want to know how much it will cost them. I'll say, 'I don't know, perhaps, £x.'

Some days they'll ask me to do it for a bit less and other days if I suggest, for instance £7,500, they'll put in £10,000 because they know they can get away with it. At times you've got to take the swings and the roundabouts. It's a terrible business really."

Commercial barrister John Jarvis, QC, says that he is only as good as his last case. "If I were to make a complete foul up in court, people would be saying: 'You know John Jarvis, what on earth has happened to him?' and it would be round the City in no time. If you are 'a name', then people expect a lot of you. Having said that, though, you can say something quite banal and it is accepted because you have said it."

Solicitor Jim Edmunds, a managing partner who specialises in asset financing and leasing, says that in the City reputation and status are everything: "Anybody who tells you otherwise is either deluding himself or he is in a very favourable position, by which I mean he is in a firm which attracts work through its name and reputation."

Part of the attraction of prestige firms like Linklaters, Allen & Overy and Slaughter and May is what he calls the IBM factor. "It's the feeling that you can't go wrong if you go to them and you can't be criticised for using them."

REPUTATION

For most City lawyers, however, "to get business you have to do cartwheels," says Edmunds wryly. "You get it by recommendation and reputation. I know most of the players in my field, which is mainly to do with asset financing and leasing, and I've known many of my clients for 20 years. In some cases, I began by advising their predecessors. Nonetheless, I can't afford to let up very much. My field is intensely competitive and if I neglect my people, my competitors will be in there in a second.

"Most banks have more than one firm of lawyers, and business which is directed mostly towards ours could quite easily be directed towards another, without anybody making any positive decisions. It just happens quietly. To maintain business, we have to be on top of it all the time."

The main worry for lawyers like Edmunds who are at the peak of their practice is that it no longer lasts until one is 65. "If you last until you are 60, you are either very lucky or jolly fit. One of my contemporaries has had at least one stroke, and he's not 50 yet. I know a number who have had heart bypasses. There's also a lot of pressure from younger people, coming up from below, competing for equity in the firm. To an extent you are on a treadmill because you have to perform and have pressures from partners to achieve targets. It's fairly ferocious."

UNDER-PERFORMERS

The younger lawyers have their own pressures, says Catrin Griffiths, the editor of Legal Business. "During a big deal, people regularly work overnight, go home, get two hours' sleep and then come back to the office. By 32 or 33, you'd better have been made partner or else. Everyone is judged by their output, and under-performers are regularly shown the door," she told The Sunday Times of London.

And so, says one female solicitor in a Chancery Lane-based firm, "when we let our hair down, we do it properly." Hence the wild behaviour which occurs, faithfully reported by Legal Business : a northern solicitor arrested for dealing Ecstasy to his clients; a City solicitor who told his colleagues he had made so much money from his last deal that he was going to have his penis cast in solid gold; and a managing partner who was discovered by a trainee solicitor in her kitchen one morning wearing only his underpants. "You should see what we had to leave out because it was too salacious," says Griffiths.

The more orthodox image of lawyers which still prevails, is that they are by nature a very conservative species and, judging by those seen on TV, "amazingly grey and faceless," according to Jim Edmunds. Many lawyers insist they are not typically given to displays of conspicuous wealth or flamboyant behaviour and the only example one senior lawyer could cite was a tax barrister who owns a Bentley. Their success enables them to do what they want to do, go where they want to go, without having too much regard for expense.

The truth probably veers between the two, depending upon the individual lawyer's maturity, emotional as well as physical, and sheer stamina. "When I'm not working really hard, which I do twelve hours a day," says a prominent solicitor, "I'm partying really hard, and I've been doing this for 25 years. I'm starting to get a bit tired."

The work-a-day lifestyle of a City lawyer has hardly changed in two decades, although three and four hour lunches are much rarer than they used to be. "The number of lunches hasn't decreased, but the amount of

Lawyers

time we spend on them is greatly reduced. Four hour boozy lunches were never usual, and mine are now down to about two a year," says one seasoned City solicitor who reserves them for out-of-town clients.

"I have one client who comes down from Glasgow and expects to be taken out to eat. We'll lunch at a place he likes, a glorified wine bar but very nice, and then we'll have a few swift libations in 'The Ship.' I don't do it as much as I did, because I'm older, and I don't want to give myself a hell of a bashing like that.

"We do everything fairly modestly because our clients perceive that they are paying for it. For instance, when I spoke to one of my clients about lunch we agreed that the deal we were going to do would pay for it and we both had a laugh about it. For, one way or another, whether we itemise the lunch or not, the cost will be in there somewhere, just as the cost of electricity is built into the bill."

If long lunches have declined, networking has developed into a fine art. One managing partner who was about to attend a dinner of 1,300 members of a finance association meeting at Grosvenor House in London described how he would work the room from 6pm to 2am.

"Going to the loo three or four times during the dinner is simply a pretext for backslapping and shaking hands on the way there and back – and seeing who is on every table."

Brinkmanship is an integral part of being a successful lawyer in every area of the profession, highly prized whether one is representing a client in the county court or the House of Lords. It typically means the lawyer refusing to accept the other side's terms, even though his client has instructed him to settle out of court.

"Let's say you've offered £100 and the other side wants £1,000. It gets close to the wire, you are 4 hours away from a court arbitration, but when the opposing solicitor asks whether you have any more money on the table, you tell him that you'll see him in court," explains a solicitor. "Fifteen minutes later he calls back and says his client is willing to settle because he doesn't want to spend money on arbitration."

PLAYING POKER

Most lawyers can cite examples of outrageous brinkmanship in which they know they are wrong on the law, do not stand a chance in court but say to the other side: "You want it, take the case to trial and the opposition melts away. They do it because they are not as smart and they haven't bothered to do their research. You would be amazed at the number of lawyers who, at times, don't know what the law is," says a young commercial lawyer.

Jim Edmunds puts this into a more kindly perspective. "Lawyers have had to become very specialised to succeed and when they take on work outside of their specialisation, which they do from time to time, they may show themselves up. A shipping solicitor, for instance, might know all about ships, but he may know very little about financing techniques when he comes to deal with me. This might make people think, therefore, that's he's a useless lawyer, which is unfair."

Lawyers

Nonetheless, City lawyers are in accord that, in too many cases, commercial clients in the provinces are being incompetently advised because their lawyers are out of their league. "I don't mean to be over-critical," says one, "but this type of lawyering is a City thing. A provincial lawyer's idea of a commercial lawyer is incorporating the local greengrocer. Certainly, their clients aren't getting the representation they should – and it costs them immensely more money."

He tells of how one transaction in the north of England dragged on for seven months when it should have taken two at most. "It was dreadful. There were at least three sets of lawyers on the other side representing two different interests, and both parties had accountants. All of them were useless."

Another City lawyer says: "What these local lawyers don't realise is that our specialisation hasn't got a lot to do with the law – it's to do with business and practice – so the whole process gets very longwinded because they are not sure what to do. Invariably in these cases they attack the bits which are obvious legally but miss those that matter commercially. They miss out the twenty or thirty pages of financial details because they don't understand them, when those are what they really need to look at."

A City lawyer is primarily concerned with applying the law so that his clients can get on with doing business. As one says: "Last November's budget (November 1996) contains many changes to various tax acts and provisions, and in the last couple of months I've been spending time with clients, thinking of ways we can still do business; or to put it more crudely, how to get round the legislation. The more complicated the legislation, the easier it is to get round. It's crazy, absolutely crazy."

UNORTHODOX METHODS

The motto in the City would appear to be win at all costs. "We will do whatever it takes within the law," says one lawyer, and that nowadays includes using private detectives. "Our clients use them and so do we, both locally and internationally. We look into people's histories to see if they have a record of having made any similar claims," he explains. "Surveillance has become part and parcel of the trade. Look at the number of 'spy' shops in and around London's South Audley Street, alone. Private investigators are employed to watch company presidents to find out who they are having lunch or dinner with, what they are talking about. If one company is competing against three others for a contract, you can believe they are going to do their homework."

So in this high-risk, high-reward culture has the gentlemanly ethos been completely eradicated? "It's still there if you look for it. There are certain firms which have never been very gentlemanly; they are a bit cut-throat and their people are a bit sharp but there are those which are not at all like that. Birds of a feather do band together," reflects one senior City partner.

Even amongst the big five firms some are perceived as more gentlemanly than the others. Jim Edmunds says: "We are supposed to be like Soames, the 'long headed

Lawyers

man' in The Forsyte Saga, the honourable person who warns you of the pitfalls but shows you a way through.

"I find that to be the case particularly now. Whereas a few years ago I was acting for people in senior positions who were older than me, now I find that I am acting for people younger than me. I can think of a couple of cases where I really feel I'm in a position of responsibility to look after senior but relatively young and inexperienced company executives who are probably operating at the limit of their abilities and experience, and I can help ensure they don't do anything wrong."

On the other hand, he says, perhaps 'gentleman' has become an embarrassing classification. "To call yourself a gentleman might well be regarded as being élitist and in our society today, you shouldn't be that. I'm mature enough not to care what they think."

LOSS LEADERS

Another change is that lawyers, who have traditionally done some work free or very cheaply to secure more work in the future, are doing far less of this. In the past, no solicitor would have thought twice about drawing up a will for a guinea or two in the knowledge that he would eventually be given the estate business. This was one of the oldest loss-leaders in the business and high street solicitors continued the custom until the meat went out of conveyancing and they could no longer afford to do it.

Doing some work for free, however, still goes on in the commercial sector. A solicitor at one of the big five firms says: "Our clients would think you were penny-pinching if they asked you for some information and you sent out a £400 bill. But if we had a client who did it regularly, we would include it in their bill sent out every six months."

The difference between now and then, says a lawyer at a smaller firm, "is that clients usually allow you to make it up on other work, although I have to say it rarely comes to pass quite like that and with such clients you find you are giving more than you get. My definition of winning is getting a bill paid."

City lawyers would accept that their profession has become very heavily commercial, but in the words of one, "if someone can make a trillion a year, let him make it." Jim Edmunds says: "If you are being successful, my attitude and the general City attitude is, well, let's make hay because it's not going to last long."

It is not unusual for barristers, either, to have a high regard for both the gentlemanly rationalist and the hard, tough million-a-year man. Gordon Pollock, QC, who is by no means the only one in the latter category, was named as the general barrister most often praised by solicitors and other barristers in a survey in the 1996-97 Chambers & Partners' Directory. "He's the best because he makes the most money," says a QC succinctly.

In the highly specialised world of company law, Richard Sykes, QC, who is singled out as its foremost practitioner, is proof that unassuming behaviour and good manners are not incompatible with six-figure earnings. "I'm not a typical barrister. I am adviser-inclined rather than advocate-inclined, and I suppose I'm quite good at finding solutions which are commercially sensi-

Lawyers

ble. I possibly have a more commercial nose." Described as the 'the experts' expert', he is atypical, too, in that he is able to maintain his No.1 position working a three-day week from 9am to 6.30p.m.

Those at the top reap the reward of trading security for independence. The most distinguished QCs may make a million or more; a larger number of slightly less prominent silks earn upwards of £700,000. But, of course, there are other motives for becoming a lawyer, and a number of the best earn a considerable income pursuing a much more humanistic course.

"Most of my work comprises legal aid cases but I've made a good living. I'm well off by a lot of standards – I can't duck that one – but I have not compromised my principles, " says one leading defence barrister, although with earnings between £100,000 and £200,000 per annum, the fact is that even exceptional criminal lawyers earn three to four times less than their civil counterparts.

PUBLIC RELATIONS

Whilst clients are attracted by a barrister's brilliant reputation it also true, says one judge, that there are different kinds of practices: "I can think of one or two people in what I call entertainment law who really are wonderful at public relations but when it gets down to doing the work, they'll leave it to one of their juniors. On the other hand, they are terribly good at getting work in."

Independence is the much prized x-factor possessed by all top barristers. "He must not be anxious to please the judges too much and he must not be a slave to his client's wishes," says Rob Webb, QC.

"Not belonging in either camp requires a certain amount of independence – and independence always brings with it a star quality because people gravitate towards someone who is independent of them."

In criminal and libel cases the barristers who do best are those with a gift for the theatrical. Dick Ferguson, QC, thinks the Irish, with their love of rhetoric, are particularly good at it. "They love the action of the court, the cut and thrust. They're not unduly concerned with the result – they see it as a game you play by the rules, and it doesn't matter much which side you're on.

"It may be because the system is one that has been imposed upon them from the outside. But the English are primarily and rightly, concerned with the result. It's not so much a matter of theatre to them – they're much more interested in getting to the truth.

"This was vividly illustrated to me by the case of the Birmingham Six. I'm still asked, 'Were they guilty?' Not just by lay people, but by lawyers,

Richard Sykes, QC

Lawyers

some of them very distinguished, as if there were some distinction for an advocate between real guilt and technical legal guilt. To me, that is appalling. My only reply is, 'How could I answer that question? I am not God.

"They are innocent. They were not convicted by due legal process. That's why I am such a great believer in the due process of law. It's not given to human beings to know whether someone is guilty or not guilty. All we can say is, 'Can you prove it in accordance with the rules of our legal system?'"

Arthur Wynn Davies, Legal Manager of The Daily Telegraph, says: "Libel is great theatre. George Carman, for instance, is just like an actor. He has tremendous reserves of nervous energy. When he's outside the court waiting, the amount of tobacco consumption is incredible. I'd say, like all successful barristers, he's driven by that little bit of fear in the gut."

Symbol of justice atop Old Bailey

At work, Carman is the essence of composure, patiently drawing out the thread of admission he will wind around his witness's neck. He is the master of cross-examination, the skill that separates the cream from the rest. "I would not want to be cross-examined by George Carman. It would be like having an operation without an anaesthetic," says a Daily Telegraph reporter. "He does nothing improper or cause pain which isn't absolutely necessary, but he is very sharp and very neat. He doesn't leave much blood on the floor, so he doesn't frighten the jury which is very important. The minute witnesses say something they should not, Carman turns it right back on them, not giving them any time to think."

A solicitor recalling the libel trial in which Jaynie Allen unsuccessfully sued Channel 4 for alleging that she had had a sexual relationship with the South African right-wing extremist Eugene Terreblanche, says: "There was a lot of seedy evidence in that case but George Carman was able in a calm, clinical way to go into the minutiae of sexual activity and utter words which can be terribly embarrassing for counsel to utter and for the jury to hear. Consequently, he didn't come across as undignified and the jury didn't feel squalid about listening attentively."

Mike Mansfield, QC says: "I don't agree that a barrister should be like a surgeon and not display any emotion as he is dissecting the case. "It's important to empathise, to get under the skin of clients to appreciate feelings. Additionally, I think a barrister has to look alive, look as if he isn't just doing his job because he's being paid for it but because he cares and because he's confident that he's right. Otherwise, the jury are going to lose faith in him.

"You have to be assertive, but that's not the same thing as being aggressive. There's a misconception that cross-examination is getting people by the throat and shaking them until their eyeballs fall out. That's ridiculous. If you want someone to talk, you have to make them feel relaxed. They have gone into court feeling overawed, anxious, perhaps even distraught. You've got to let them feel that you understand or, at least, that you want to understand.

"Obviously, there may come a point when you have to say you don't believe them but there are ways to do this. You can say, 'I do have to suggest something rather different. Could it have happened like this…?' Then you pause and wait for them to answer. If they want a break, you give them a break because they have to answer eventually. You just go on asking the question and often they make concessions. But being gently persistent is not the same as being unpleasant.

"I am aware that I am known as a 'hatchet man' but basically it's a misconception. Occasionally, you do get a witness who is arrogant, who insists that his memory is superhuman, or who is covering something up, and then you have to go for him. But then that's fair game because he's not playing the game anyway. He is not telling the truth, so you don't let him off the hook."

WOOING THE JURY
Charm is often mentioned as a prominent characteristic of distinguished lawyers. "Dick Ferguson plays the parts of good cop, bad cop," says one court reporter. "But the jury don't hold the nasty moments against him because he comes across as a genial, charming man.

Unlike many lawyers he's very good at explaining things to them without being pompous. You really need that kind of lawyer if the client is someone the jury wouldn't be expected to like."

Pomposity and being out of touch with the average juryman have definitely lost cases, says barrister Quincy Whitaker.

"I haven't been a barrister so long that I can't recognise words that people don't normally use. The longer you're in this job, the greater the tendency to fall into legal language because you use it with one another. But top barristers always remember to be down-to-earth. I once heard a lawyer saying, 'Members of the jury, this man is a mountebank'. I looked at their faces, and it was clear that several of them didn't know what the word meant. They were not only bewildered but embarrassed. How that barrister thought he was helping his client, I can't imagine."

PRESENTING THE CASE

Playing to a jury is very different from addressing an audience of one. Barrister Matthew Reeve says: "A criminal trial progresses at the pace of the slowest juror. It can be a very rhythmic performance which steers a course between feeding too many facts to the jury or too few, and has a degree of dramatic intensity. But in the commercial civil world, where you are presenting a case to the judge, you have to acknowledge the pressure on him to get through his work.

"One of the things he's looking for is a convenient

Lawyers

packaging of the most relevant facts in the case with the most logical argument – the one that won't be found wanting on appeal. If you can also throw in a bit of entertainment, as the head of my chambers Rob Webb does, then you are a very special advocate."

MAXWELL CASE

A barrister, like an actor, is only as good as his material. Hence close co-operation with the solicitor is vital. When solicitor Keith Oliver took on the Kevin Maxwell case, he teamed up not only with his barristers Alun Jones and Clare Montgomery but also with his client. "We decided that the only way to get away from the pressures

of the case was to stay with Kevin for a few weeks. We got together at breakfast and stayed at the table until dinnertime. "Traditionally, at the criminal bar, the solicitor would take a detailed proof of evidence from the client giving his account of every aspect of the case. But this was never going to be the kind of case in

Maxwell case lawyer, Keith Oliver which you delivered a

60 to 70 page proof to counsel, who would shut himself away with it for a couple of days and come back with a series of precise, erudite questions. So we had to think of an approach that would fit this unusual situation."

He says that the strategy they adopted was unorthodox. "On the first day of the trial, Alun Jones told the court that Kevin Maxwell would be giving evidence. In my experience it is unique for counsel to throw his cards on the table like that, and I'm sure it had an effect on the way the jury perceived Kevin. Michael Briggs, QC, was also very important in creating a favourable impression of Kevin. The day after Kevin complied with a court order to surrender his passport, Michael Briggs got it back so that Kevin could go to New York in the early stages of the case. What Michael Briggs achieved was indefinable but fundamental to the case, as it demonstrated that Kevin Maxwell could be relied upon to keep his word."

DON'T SUE

Though the star lawyers who get most attention are the barristers, with their field days in court, clients appreciate not only the lawyers who get them acquitted but those who keep them far from the court-room door. Solicitor Sean Gates' advice to anyone about to sue is: "Don't. It's the worst thing you can do. Try to solve your problem some other way."

Even so, he says, "You can give people all the good advice you like, but there are always people who want to get out on the jousting field and see blood, and assume it won't be theirs."

Lawyers

John Eastman, the lawyer who represents Paul McCartney in his multi-million-pound deals, put it another way: "I do not believe in putting my client's fate in the hands of total strangers. A judge and jury are total strangers."

Chapter Six

DIRECTING THE ACTION

Top judges in Britain have become third-age rebels. They outmanoeuvred and outflanked the former Tory government in the past two years with skills a matador would envy – notwithstanding their average age of 60. Whether they maintain this role under the Labour government is the subject of riveting speculation amongst the legal profession.

The time-worn, vicious swipe that judges dwell in ivory towers loses its sting when one considers that they opposed the Conservatives, who were forced to compromise on the down-to-earth issues of minimum sentences, asylum seekers and police bugging. According to BBC legal correspondent Joshua Rozenburg, they spoke up because Labour, then in opposition, seemed reluctant to do so.

Due to extremely unusual and outspoken criticism on policy from the massed ranks of the judiciary, the minimum sentences bill was modified. It allowed judges to impose a lesser sentence 'in the interests of justice'. Senior judges ruled that it was illegal for the government to withdraw benefits from asylum seekers whose applications to stay in the UK had not yet been determined, and they won a change in the police 'bugging' bill stipulating that authorisation must be obtained from a judge, not just a chief constable, when the police want to tap 'phones.

There has also been an explosion of judicial review cases, overturning all sorts of decisions made by central and local government and financial regulatory bodies in the last few years, making it one of the most fashionable areas of law in which to practise. "Indeed, the way the judiciary has taken on the government makes the Bar appear reactionary in comparison," says radical barrister Quincy Whitaker.

Another barrister says that the judges' independent stance in the 1990's follows decades of toeing the government line, particularly in the late1960's and 1970's, which coincided with a number of grave miscarriages of justice, some of which are only now coming to light.

'JUDGE-ITIS'

Despite praise for the judiciary's current collective show of strength from those within the legal profession, many lawyers, clients and the public view some individual judges as proof of the principle that people rise to the limits of their capacities, and then a bit more. No lawyer questioned for this book could explain why otherwise some good, even excellent, lawyers undergo a complete personality change or become incompetent when they take to the Bench. It is called 'judge-itis.'

"I do wonder what happens to these very sensible barristers who go mad when they get on the High Bench," says a long-time barrister's clerk. "Whether it's the power,

Directing the Action

I don't know, but they suddenly change for the worse. The opinions you know they held at the Bar are sometimes completely at odds with the decisions they are making as judges.

"I said to one barrister whom I've known for twenty years and who was about to become a judge: 'Don't get like some of the others.' He told me to keep calling him 'Andrew'. There are some who insist that you call them Mr. Justice So-and-So, even when you have been on first-name terms with them for years and years."

Bouts of overweening self-regard on the bench, or ignorance of sex practices and pop stars, resulting in judges being ridiculed by the press, disguise far deeper concerns. Partisan judges, who violate the basic tenet that justice should be done and be seen to be done, are the bane of lawyers' lives and have, in their view, seriously damaged the public's faith in the legal system.

Dick Ferguson, QC, was involved in the penultimate appeal of the 'Birmingham Six', at which Lord Chief Justice Lane uttered the famous words: "The longer this hearing has gone on the more convinced this court has become that the verdict of the jury (in the original trial) was correct."

Ferguson says: "What happened in those 'miscarriage-of-justice' cases, and there were a number of them, not all Irish, was that the establishment, as represented by the top echelons of the legal profession, refused to countenance the possibility of error by the lower courts. Instead of approaching the appeals with an open mind, they determined to uphold the convictions.

Lawyers

"Even when the evidence had reached a stage where it should have been obvious to them that it was time to admit failure, they still tried to cling to the convictions. And it was only when the convictions were finally wrested from them that they gave up. Of course, that much publicised delay has done irreparable damage to the image of our legal system."

Bias is no less invidious at county court level. Barrister Jacqueline Perry recalls representing a man seeking custody of his children, as their mother had a history of abandoning them and then reclaiming them for short periods. "The county court judge, however, made it clear during the early part of the case that he believed a child's place was with his mother and, no surprise, ruled in her favour. My client felt with good reason that he hadn't had a proper hearing. This is an example of a judge who had made up his mind and wasn't prepared to listen to anything else."

Lawyers, understandably critical of such prejudiced attitudes, are divided on whether or not the composition of the judiciary is partly responsible.

One leading QC, in an establishment set, says the English judiciary is 'a classic oligarchy', a form of government in which power is vested in a few. "You rise only if you conform to the prevailing attitudes of the group. I think there is a prevailing tone that says junior judges have to conform to social, or legal, or even political attitudes of the majority of judges in order to get promoted. So if, for example, you are appointed High Court judge, and want to become a Lord Justice and sit in the Court of

Appeal or House of Lords, then you do become influenced by their attitudes."

STATUS QUO

Knowing that one's fellow judge is shaped by the same culture, values and perceptions, that he can be counted on to maintain the status quo, evidently remains an important criterion in selecting most senior judges - who are picked by invitation only.

Mr. Justice Rodger Bell is one of ten senior judges currently on the Bench, who have emerged from 1 Crown Office Row, a set of chambers which, he says, has, "produced an awful lot of judges." "Obviously, a part of that is if former members, now judges, are 'sounded out' about someone who is coming up behind, and they think he is good material, they won't hesitate to say so. The other factor is, and it's guess work only, if you have a number of judges from a certain set of chambers who have, therefore, all been brought up in the same ethos, they may think that anyone else from that same set is likely to be a safe pair of hands. And being a safe pair of hands probably counts for quite a lot nowadays."

Mike Mansfield, QC, has long believed that, "a system in which judges are chosen from about one per cent of

As of April 1997, judges' annual salaries are as follows:	
Lord Chief Justice:	£138,165
Court of Appeal judges:	£122,415
High Court judges:	£108,192
Circuit judges:	£79,667

the population cannot have the confidence of the community." He advocates they should come from all walks of life. He would prefer a judiciary modelled more on European lines in which being a judge entails going from university to a judicial college and is seen as a long-term career. "In Britain, becoming a judge is viewed as some kind of golden handshake - a third age career."

But there are many barristers who do not believe it is necessary to have a judiciary which reflects the community in order for justice to be done, and seen to be done. Rob Webb, QC says: "I'd rather have a detached, mature person, experienced in the ways of courts, trying my cases than I would somebody who came as a representative of a point-of-view, race or particular culture."

Most High Court judges are selected from the QC ranks of the Bar and the remainder from the ranks of circuit judges. Solicitors can be appointed, but this happens so rarely that when Arthur Marriott and Dr. Lawrence Collins were appointed to the High Court Bench in March this year, it was national news.

Barrister Daphne Loebl says: "To the public, who becomes a QC is important because this country's lawmakers are appointed from their ranks. So, if you want them to be more representative, you either have to change that method of selecting judges and divorce it from the QC selection process, or you have to make sure that QC selection is fairer and get more ethnic minorities and women into silk."

The judiciary is still almost exclusively public school, Oxbridge-educated, white and male. Of the 129 judges in the upper courts, there are just seven women, six of them on the High Court Bench and only one, Dame Elizabeth Butler-Sloss, sitting in the Court of Appeal.

Mansfield says Lord Mackay, former Lord Chancellor, disagreed 'absolutely and entirely' that the judiciary should reflect the community. His objective was to have at most, "maybe ten to twelve women on the High Court Bench in 50 years time – perhaps."

The present Lord Chancellor, Lord Irvine of Lairg, is more diplomatic but his message does not seem to differ intrinsically from that of his predecessor. He said recently: "It would not be appropriate to set quotas for the number of women on the Bench, or even estimate the percentage of women judges in so many years' time. That would be pure guesswork.

"The number of women judges is increasing, and every indication is that this will continue. There are large numbers of very good candidates for judicial office, both male and female, and the competition for appointment is very fierce.

A fairer profession for women?

Lawyers

"Those who do succeed, do so on their merits," he says. "I would like to see more women in the judiciary and I am determined to see that, when they do apply for judicial appointment, they are treated fairly. What is encouraging to me is that, taking the latest round of assistant recorder appointments, 16% of applicants were female, and 22% of those who were successful were female. These figures are encouraging, seen in the context of the number of eligible practitioners with the necessary seniority."

At circuit court level, where lawyers can apply for a judgeship, there is a four-year waiting list. "If you fill in your form now, they may wave at you before your retirement and think about having you," says one female barrister. "A lot of it is lip service: 'We do want you but we are not sure how to accommodate you'. It's a depressing profession in many ways."

One starts off as an assistant recorder, having passed an interview given by the Lord Chancellor's department and a QC or judge, and progresses to recorder (a voluntary judge who sits in at Crown Court hearings). A recorder is qualified to apply to become a circuit judge but need be given no reason if the application is turned down.

As for the superior courts, a female barrister says drily: "I've not noticed any change in the upper echelons. There is, in effect, a judges' club. For those within it, it's a question of 'when' they become a judge; for most of us, it's a question of 'if'."

The insiders' perspective is best summed up by a now

retired High Court judge, Sir William Macpherson of Cluny, the 27th hereditary chief of the clan of Macphersons, who once told Mr Justice Bell: "The great joy about the Bar is you get the opportunity to have three careers; as a junior barrister, as a silk and as a judge, if it all goes well. Whereas most people don't get that opportunity to change their career."

Sir Brian Neill, a former Court of Appeal judge, says the perception that judicial selection is deliberately in one's own image is 'a sad one' and that time will inevitably change the make-up of the judiciary. "When I came to the Bar in 1949, the really clever women didn't go on. There was one woman who practised for a short time and, in my view, would be in the Court of Appeal or House of Lords if she had gone on with it. But she went into academia.

"Today women are practising and I would like to ask anybody who says, 'Why aren't there more women?' Please tell me, 'Who would you select?' I don't see very many women, because they tend to be criminal practitioners, but I see quite a number from the family courts and in employment cases, and the majority are extremely good. There are other women, in their 30's and 40's, who will certainly come through the system in the next ten years.

"As for ethnic minorities, they have found it difficult until recently to do civil litigation, such as commercial cases. They have concentrated very largely on immigration work and, perhaps, criminal cases. They aren't possibly seen enough by senior judges, so it's more difficult for them to be selected."

Unfortunately, Appeal Court Judge, Lord Justice Rose, let slip at last year's Association of Women Lawyers Conference that he could think of a couple of female barristers who had been promoted beyond their abilities and, had they been men, would not have made QC.

He immediately apologised, but says one female lawyer: "It is more than a little worrying. One wonders how many senior judges go around with this idea in their heads." In an effort to change hearts and minds, the Association of Women Barristers invited L.J. Rose to its annual dinner this year. He accepted. "To be fair, he is now willing to enter a dialogue with us to see a different point of view," says a committee member

SPEAKING OUT.

Judges today - dinosaurs apart - are aware that the public is more and more suspicious of the legal system and that they need to provide information and reassurance. At a recent conference of the Commonwealth Judges' and Magistrates' Association, they were told: "It is simply no longer sensible to remain silent when so much attention, much of it highly critical, is focused on the courts and judicial process. In the absence of any reply, it would be assumed against the judges either that they were so arrogant and complacent as to believe they could ignore criticism, or that they had no good answer to it."

It was pointed out to them that the public believes that judges are far softer on crime than they in fact are. For, according to a study conducted by the Nuffield Foundation, half the public think that 50% or fewer convicted rapists are sent to prison whereas the true figure is 91%, and that 20% or fewer convicted muggers are sent to prison whereas the correct figure is 50%.

Judges, however, remain extremely wary about speaking out. "One is less inhibited about speaking out than in the past," says Sir Brian. "But I think it is very dangerous to answer the question: 'Why did you decide that case in that way?' I'm not saying there aren't exceptional circumstances but I don't think you should enter into a public debate about a case after you have given your decision in court.

"In the past ten years I have given a number of controversial decisions in terms of popular opinion, because in this job you are bound to have some very hot potatoes. I realise that a number of decisions have been criticised. But what do you do at the next stage? If you don't speak out, you are liable to be charged with being aloof and arrogant; on the other hand, there really is no satisfactory way of explaining a decision or qualifying what you have already decided.

"You can hardly expect to be given ten minutes of TV air time to explain your side, and if you wrote a letter to The Times you would simply be paraphrasing what you have already stated. I think judges are far more aware of public reaction and have become more careful in what we call 'judges' remarks."

But though there is the temptation for a judge to keep his head beneath the parapet, one of the judiciary's oft used phrases, Sir Brian says: "I think it's impossible to do so. You've got to make decisions which you recognise are going to be unpopular with some people, if you think they are right."

Dick Ferguson, QC, says: "Once you become a High Court judge, you inevitably deprive yourself of a measure of independence, because cases will come along which you would be inclined to decide in a certain way. But because you know that a decision may create a public hue and cry, you do the politic thing.

"Tension is inevitable between doing what is right and proper and being a safe pair of hands. I think you are bound to err on the side of conservatism because you don't want to be the one who comes up with a decision that is unpopular with the media. You don't want to be the one, perhaps, who is publicly seen as out of step with your colleagues.

"The difficulty is that the law is not a set of rules cast in concrete. It has to change as society changes if it is not to diverge too much from justice. People's ideas of what is right and wrong change, and the law has to take account of that, but the law can't change too quickly. People must know that what they legally do today isn't going to be declared a crime tomorrow. Judges are berated for being behind public opinion, but the law is always, to an extent, behind public opinion. It has to be, to make sure it's changing the right way. So it's a question of trying always to bridge the gap."

The matter of rape, for instance, which has been the subject of much media outrage, is a good illustration of the difference between the law and the public view of justice. As far as the public is concerned, says Ferguson, all rapists should be castrated, but some receive lenient sentences due to powerful mitigating factors. "Of course, the press who love to have a go at judges get hold of these cases and then lambaste judges for being too lenient. What I am saying is that it defeats the object of the exercise if judges have to impose sentences right across the board, irrespective of the circumstances."

There is division among the legal profession about whether there are different degrees of rape. Some take the view that there is a difference between a woman raped by a stranger as she walks home and one who says 'no' to her date at the last minute. Others believe this distinction to be false.

While the law does try to distinguish between very bad cases and those which are wholly unacceptable but are not at the top of the scale, lawyers admit that they are very careful about saying so in public. Judges are also acutely aware that decisions they made in the past and which were not criticised might well be now.

STATUS

Despite such dilemmas and weighty responsibilities, the combination of worldly honours, status and a desire to improve the administration of justice will always have its allure. "I like to think that the status is not important to me, but that can't be right because, obviously it's important to anyone to a certain extent," says one High Court judge. "I still think it's a bit of distinction without going overboard. I feel a sense of duty, too. Besides, many of my friends and family would never have forgiven me if they'd heard I'd been invited and said no." (One long-time judge's clerk says: "I have never yet met a judge whose wife wanted the job more than he did.")

Nonetheless, more and more QCs are declining judgeships – once a rare decision – because of the huge drop in income. Mr Justice Bell was approached twice about becoming a circuit court judge, and says candidly: "I was not interested, and there's no mystery about the reason. I have a reasonably large family and would have taken a considerable drop in earnings. Becoming a High Court judge hasn't entailed as great a drop."

Even so, the successful lawyers of today are less likely to be tempted by a High Court judge's salary of £108,192 when they can earn double, triple, or more in private practice.

The isolation, which increases with seniority and contrasts with the 'clubbiness' of the Bar, is also a disincentive. "Apart from being in court with my colleagues, there may have been days when I would not have seen anybody," says Sir Brian, who retired two years early but continues to sit as a part-time judge at the Court of Appeal, although he no longer presides. "In my room at the Royal Courts of Justice, if I was not writing, I was reading, so it was lonely in that sense.

Many lawyers balk, too, at the idea of having to make judgments. Sir Brian says: "I know an extremely able criminal lawyer who didn't want to become a judge. He often prosecuted, but he didn't like the idea of sentencing."

In contrast, those barristers who do decide to become judges prize the idea of having the final say on a case: "Arguing a case can give you an amazing number of intellectual challenges," recalls Sir Brian, "but it can be frustrating never to see the result. I began to think I should like to decide something."

Another reason is simply the desire for a change. One High Court judge says: "I was doing mostly medical negligence and personal injury cases: cerebral palsy babies, paraplegics, brain damage victims, but much of my work was to do with working out the amount of damages. I was dealing with the same issues and arguments, schedules and counter-schedules, and one can get a bit jaded."

YOUNGER JUDGES

The fact that Britain's most powerful lawmakers regard judgeship as a third career which they tend, in the main, to take up in their 50's, is increasingly out of step with public opinion in Europe and the US. New York Judge, Joan Carey, who practices in Manhattan, once told Mike Mansfield: "For quite a few years the attitude in this country has been that being a judge should not be a retiring position. People should bring to it a certain youthful quality and interest in things other than going to clubs and having sabbaticals."

Until the 1960's British judges were able to continue indefinitely; now superior judges appointed before 1995 must retire at 75 years, and those appointed since have to retire at 70 . At the highest level, in the House of Lords, it means that no one over the age limit can sit for particular cases, even as a part-time judge, however expert.

But a surprising number of young barristers, radical as well as establishment, maintain that age has little to do with ability and should be no bar to being a judge. Barrister Quincy Whitaker says: "I'd rather come before a good judge of 70 than an incompetent one of 50.

The sign of a good judge, according to John Jarvis, QC, is that he is able to cut to the heart of the problem, and show clearly and succinctly how and why he reaches his decisions; all the while making the losing side feel his point of view has been fully taken into account. "I know a loser is always going to be disgruntled, but at least he feels you have seen his point of view."

INTIMIDATION

Predictably, the most unpopular judges are those who are farthest removed from this ideal. Capricious and irascible behaviour by judges comes in for much censure. A survey in the trade magazine 'Legal Business' reports a lawyer saying of Lord Justice Jeremiah Harman: "If he takes a dislike to your face then God help you."

Mr Justice Ian Kennedy is purported to be equally intimidating. Worse still, it seems, are judges who dither. The magazine found the most disliked judge on the Bench was Mr Justice Peter Cresswell. "If his wife puts out two bowls of cereal for him," one lawyer was quoted as saying, "he never gets to work."

The judges' clerks who are, in the main, retired members of the police, army and navy say that those on the Bench are not as cohesive a bunch, or as inhuman, as they are portrayed. One clerk recalls: "My judge was once approached by one of his particularly egocentric colleagues who wanted to accompany him to the annual induction of new members of the Bar at Westminster Abbey. I heard my judge mutter: 'Over my dead body'."

They are able to cite instances of snobbery which involve judges not acknowledging their own clerks in public, or refusing to speak directly to a solicitor. "Some judges won't speak to solicitors at all; they insist on talking to barristers," says a judge's clerk. "Other judges will speak to a solicitor only if a barrister is unavailable. It's pure snobbery."

Those guilty of such behaviour might care to remem-

Lawyers

ber that one of their most exceptional and distinguished Court of Appeal judges, Lord Widgery, started off as a solicitor. He also had a sharp sense of humour. When a guest attending the induction of new members of the Bar commented: "No court is sitting today. No justice of any kind is being meted out," Lord Widgery instantly replied, "And no injustice either."

Chapter Seven

BOWING OUT

A very few successful lawyers exit spectacularly in public disgrace, quite a few become politicians, many more take on consultancies or non-executive directorships. But most retire quietly to enjoy their accumulated wealth, which comes in many-splendid forms: a country estate in France, a Scottish castle, a priceless African art collection in Palm Springs or an Onassis-style yacht in the Florida Keys.

At the very least, says recruitment consultant David Woolfson, they will play golf, collect antiques or belong to a sailing/yachting/rowing/gentlemen's/club or two. "We are talking about the top lawyers, and they retire very, very comfortably indeed."

But not always without a backward glance, it seems. "I see a lot of people who have retired, and they miss the status," says an eminent QC. "For 25 years people have been coming to them for advice and then, suddenly, nobody does. Nobody cares what they think any more."

It is enough to deflate the most pompous ego, pomposity being a trait to which the profession is particularly prone because, says one lawyer: "You need to have enormous self-confidence to do the job at all – and enormous

Lawyers

self-confidence can always tip over into enormous self-regard."* Or as barrister Matthew Reeve puts it: "It is so intoxicating, being paid to speak."

Causing a scandal, of course, is the most extreme method of avoiding affluent oblivion. In 1991 Sir Allan Green, QC, then Director of Public Prosecutions, fell from grace from a great height, after he was stopped by police for alleged kerb-crawling at King's Cross in London.

The story made national newspaper headlines for days, and he resigned his post. The police did not recommend that he be prosecuted, however, and he did not incur any professional sanctions. His marriage broke up under the strain and, tragically, his wife committed suicide. But Green, a popular and able man, was viewed with sympathy by his peers and returned to a successful private practice.

A senior lawyer and a friend of Green's says: "Sexual peccadilloes do not affect a man's ability to be a member of the Bar. What they do affect is his ability to be sitting in judgment as to whether people should be prosecuted or not. And that's the distinction which Allan Green recognised. He resigned as DPP because, although he had committed no criminal offence, he said it would be inap-

---

* In the US, reputations and careers are ruined by, "scandal, incompetence, making a fool of yourself and turning on your client," says Professor Robert Post. "An example of the latter is the lawyer who represented O.J. Simpson and then publicly turned on him after the case. It is never a good thing to do."

propriate for him to determine whether anybody else should be prosecuted if, say, they were found loitering at King's Cross."

COURTING TROUBLE

The charges which cause barristers to end up before a disciplinary committee usually involve professional misconduct of some kind. "The committee is very hot on criminal convictions; for instance, they take drink-driving offences very seriously. Bankruptcy and repeated complaints about negligence also come in for much censure," says one barrister.

More commonly, barristers are caught faking legal aid claims or misleading the court. One was banned from practising for two years after making inflammatory public remarks at the time of the Brixton riots; another was disbarred altogether after ignoring a warning not to describe himself, falsely, as a QC. Others have been suspended for lying to a judge.

A senior barrister was suspended for three months after saying he could not be in court because of a professional commitment. This is usually taken to mean that he has been asked to sit in the High Court or Court of Appeal. Unfortunately for him, he was seen on television attending a board meeting concerning his private business interests.

The disciplinary hearings are held in camera, but although the deliberations are secret, the results are published in the Bar's trade magazine, 'Counsel.' "I don't know what, if any, effect this has on barristers' reputations or their business," says a young barrister, "because solicitors, who provide barristers with work, do not read it."

The suspicion amongst solicitors that barristers, despite their 'holier than thou' attitude, are not immune to financial temptation but find it easier to cover up, is borne out by the case of a former head of a provincial chambers. Having run up serious gambling debts, he embezzled money from his own set and was found out by the other members. In order to avoid a scandal, which would have damaged the reputation of the entire set, leading to severe loss of earnings or even its collapse, he was made to leave quietly and replaced by an irreproachable QC. The matter never reached the Bar Council.

HANDS IN THE TILL

Solicitors though, it has to be said, are the ones with the means and opportunity. With the decline of business during the recent recession combined with the loss of their conveyancing monopoly in the 80's, many found the funds in their client accounts too tempting to resist. The result , says senior partner John Clitheroe, who sits on the Solicitors' Disciplinary Tribunal, is "the biggest upsurge of criminality amongst the solicitors profession which has been seen for a century or more."

Clitheroe's personal view, based on the number of 'horrifying cases' that come before him, is that solicitor crime is prompted more by desperation than by greed. "What happens is something like this: I am living in a village or small country town, and I am a pillar of society along with three or four other solicitors and two or three doctors, and we are the élite. I live in a six-bedroom house near the golf club, of which I am a member. My three children go to fee-paying schools, and my wife rides and is a member of the Women's Institute. She's got to have a new dress each week for various functions. Suddenly my income is halved. I'll have to go home and say to my wife, 'I'm sorry, darling, you've got to give up your riding and your car and stop buying clothes, the kids have got to go to state schools, and we won't be able to entertain or go on holiday'. And a lot of them can't bring themselves to do it. Or they do, and their wife says, 'Don't be stupid, go and earn the money'.

"A lot of these people feel they have been betrayed. They grew up thinking of the law as an honourable vocation, like the church or army. They worked hard to build a practice and felt that they should be looked up to because they were supposed to be, and should have been, a reputable representative of what, I suppose, are good, middle-class virtues. And now they feel that their living and status are being taken away from them and they're going to fight tooth and claw to defend themselves."

The first false step is usually is a minor one which Clitheroe describes as the £500 syndrome. "The solicitor might have a £500 telephone bill, and he has a client who owes him £1,000. So he takes £500 of the client's money, thinking that when the client pays what he owes, he will replace it. Then the client fails to pay him, or even goes bust, and meanwhile another bill arrives…

Lawyers

"What solicitors have had to appreciate is that the police are really enjoying life at the moment because they are prosecuting more solicitors than ever before. The man who has been cross-examining and casting doubt on their evidence for the past 20 years, is suddenly the man in the dock for aiding and abetting a mortgage fraud."

In a basic mortgage fraud, a solicitor pretends to handle the sale of a property and applies to ten or twelve banks or building societies for mortgages. He then accepts all the offers and takes the money. The fraud will eventually be discovered by the Land Registry office when it receives several registrations for one property, but since it can take up to 90 days to process applications, the perpetrator will have had plenty of time to disappear.

Other cases involve sole practitioners who, in league with a surveyor estate agent or bank manager, swear the property is worth more than its actual value, and pocket the difference. Consequently, some banks now refuse to do business with sole practitioners.

GREED AND DISGRACE

Greed, however, and not desperation is the motivating factor behind the really huge embezzlements and frauds. Solicitor Guy Lucas was struck off the solicitors' roll in 1992 after being arrested with 18 others in connection with Britain's biggest ever mortgage fraud, which led to the loss of £100 million. Equally controversial is the case of Hilary Stone, a former senior partner with a city law firm. She was struck off and is under investigation by police after £600,000 of the proceeds of Westminster Council's right-to-buy scheme disappeared.* Such is the complexity of these two cases that neither has yet been tried, although Lucas' trial may be heard later this year.

In January this year, Peter Hedworth, a solicitor who masterminded a sophisticated £1 million mortgage and property fraud, was jailed for six years, following a trial lasting almost five months. He used the money from building societies and clients' accounts to fund the creation of a 'farmland paradise' in the Lake District, where he planned to breed rare sheep and cattle.

The Solicitors' Disciplinary Tribunal holds all its hearings in public, and a news agency feeds the national and regional media with relevant cases.

"A lot of firms try to prevent any story from being written because of a concern that the local press will try and crucify their reputation. In many cases it just isn't fair," says Zoe Etherington of the Office for the Supervision of Solicitors. "So if they have been co-operative, and we have found no evidence that anyone else was involved, then we are at pains to make this clear to the press, and we try to temper the story."

Fraud and dishonesty were worst in the late 1980s and early 1990s, according to the Office for the Supervision

---

* It was renamed the Homes-for-Votes Programme after the council's secret policy of selling homes in key marginal wards to affluent professionals on the assumption that such newcomers would be more likely to vote Conservative than council tenants.

of Solicitors, and in 1994 it had to pay an unprecedented £29 million compensation to victims. Thus the Compensation Fund levy, which every solicitor has to pay, soared from £365 in 1991 to £1,045 in 1992 and 1993.

Etherington of the O.S.S., explains: "These figures reflect what had been happening in the early1990s. Since then our figures seem to mirror a trend that fraud at its worst has been and gone, or so one hopes. Because of sums accruing in the compensation fund, where we've collected more than we've paid out, the amount solicitors will have to pay next year will go down to £100. We are aware, though, that it takes only a couple of exceptional cases to bounce the amount up again."

Compensation funds are paid when there is no other resort – when, for example, a sole practitioner in a firm is dishonest or all the partners are dishonest. If most of the partners are honest, they are insured against the dishonesty of a single solicitor by their indemnity fund. But the Solicitors' Indemnity Fund admitted, in a shock announcement in June 1997, that it will need £454 million more than originally projected to satisfy negligence and dishonesty claims arising between 1989 and 1997. Consequently, solicitors face a huge hike in their premiums to bridge the gap.

Some high street firms predict that the tens of thousands of pounds extra they would have to contribute would put them out of business. While the Law Society is seeking other ways of making up some of the deficit, there is a huge investigation into how the fund managed to underestimate the cost of claims to such an extent.

Bowing Out

Being overzealous can lead to quick departure from the profession. Lawyers have at times gone too far to help their clients: forging passports for them or, like one solicitor who was struck off for perjury, certifying the authenticity of false documents in his eagerness to win a case.

Solicitor Keith Oliver says the current system is at fault by, in some cases, intensifying the desire to win to a dangerous degree. "In Britain, lawyers are not automatically allowed to take a case on the basis that their fee will be a percentage of the winnings, as they can in the US. Instead, the English have adopted a typically Anglo-Saxon compromise to contingency fees.

"Subject to the client's prior consent, if a lawyer wins a certain type of case, he can double his costs; if he loses, he gets nothing. Now, if you have a situation where the lawyer has a financial interest in the outcome that goes beyond a reasonable return for his legal expertise, in my view that can, in some cases, lead to a breaking or pushing at the outer limits of the rules."

This is one of the objections now being levelled against plans by Britain's Labour Government to save £300 million on legal aid expenditure by introducing a 'no-win, no-fee' system in all civil proceedings with the exception of family cases. It offers the prospect of successful lawyers earning much higher income but, conversely, a string of adverse verdicts could put a legal team in financial difficulty.

It is a sad fact that even under the present system some 30% of QCs fail because they find themselves competing against a pool of far more experienced barristers than they were as juniors. Their fees rise to match their title but they then have to prove that they represent value for money. Consequently, says Rob Webb QC: "If you charge more and are not worth more, you get nothing."

What is more, there is no way QCs can wind their career backwards: the letters after their name can be taken away for misbehaviour, but they cannot be given up. As QCs who are out of their depth have discovered, far from being a licence to print money, silk can be a one-way ticket to oblivion.

Then there are those barristers who simply become unfashionable. "How do you tell them?," asks a clerk. "We had a barrister who did planning work and was very successful until the last five years, when the market-place changed. He's what I call a true gentleman, low key and calm. But clients no longer want lawyers like that. They want gung-ho types who are brash and aggressive, even though they don't win any more cases than those who are perceived as old-fashioned. It reached a point when he wasn't earning enough money to pay chambers' expenses, and we suggested he become a circuit court judge. He didn't want to, he just retired. It was very sad."

Solicitors' careers can also decline undramatically. "There is always a 'make-or-break' case on the way up," says an observant solicitor, "but there is rarely one on the way down. What's far more likely to happen is that the business simply goes away from you; the director of the company with whom you have a good relationship is fired or retires, and that's the last you see of that company which has been providing most of your work for the past dozen years.

"Meanwhile, there are other, younger guys in the firm ready to take your place. They are bringing in clients, and may leave the firm, taking those clients with them if they are not made partner in a reasonable time. What happens then is that the pack turns on its weakest member; the partners pay him off and tell him to go."

"This is not an option open to sets, says a clerk: "Barristers are self-employed, so it's difficult to get rid of them."

KNOWING WHEN TO STOP

So when is it time to go? "I'd say a major sign of decline is when you start talking about individual cases. Rumpole was always referring to the 'Penge Bungalow murders' as his great moment. Talking about past cases means the high-spot of your career is over," says one QC, only half in jest.

Mike Mansfield, QC says: "The obvious answer is when you can no longer carry on and give the service you have been giving. Often, you are the worst judge of that because you can kid yourself that you have done a great job. Compulsory retirement? I'm not sure. I am not an ageist. In terms of general practice, it is possible to go on.

"One nonagenarian I know does the odd case and makes no more mistakes than the rest of us. One can only hope that, when it is time, somebody who is a close

Lawyers

friend, clerk or partner will be able say 'I think it is time you eased-up'."

Chapter Eight

THE FUTURE

There are some 800,000 lawyers in the US and they make up about half the total number in the world. In the face of such mighty legal muscle, it is hardly surprising that the rest of the species have fixed their gaze westwards, wondering if they are looking at their future.

The prospect of the British legal system being engulfed by the American way, and its lawyers in time becoming indistinguishable from their cousins across the Atlantic, might sound far-fetched, but it is considered a very real possibility by practitioners here. There are currently 62 US law firms with offices in London, comprising almost half the entire number of foreign legal firms in the capital.

One senior solicitor at a UK practice recalls how some of his partners resisted the recruitment of an American, despite the firm being international. "They argued that our systems were different, that English people who were qualified had applied, and that this was the beginning of the end, a take-over of our system by theirs." It is a slight case of xenophobic over-reaction, perhaps, but an indication, nonetheless, of the high level of emotion US

Lawyers

encroachment arouses.

At the heart of such concern, even fear, is that the law will cease to be a profession and come to be viewed and run strictly as a business. Lawyer Henry Hecht, who is a lecturer at the University of California, Berkeley, says: "The practice of law is driven by economics in a way that it was not when I started practising 24 years ago. It is extraordinarily competitive."

This is reflected in the type of books The American Bar Association currently publishes: 'Alternative Billing Strategies the Sequel', 'Billing Innovations: New Win-Win Ways to end Hourly Billing' and, hot off the press, 'The Lawyer's Guide to the Internet', all of them detailing strategies to attract clients with the emphasis on marketing.

Lawyer and author, John Osborn

"The ability to bring in business is an incredibly important issue at many firms these days," observes Hecht. "So if you want to succeed at the firm, you must bring in clients." How to achieve this, he adds, is the underlying focus of many law firm discussions.

The Future

This attitude is a direct consequence of the globalisation of corporate American business in general, and of accountancy firms in particular. Such multi-nationals argue that, by merging practices, they offer their clients a more comprehensive and standard service.

"It's rather like going to the Hilton Hotel," says a Law Society spokesman. "You know what you are getting because it's the same everywhere in the world. So when commercial clients ask their accountants to refer a lawyer to them, they know that, wherever they are in the world, the procedure will be familiar and the standards will be more or less the same."

A WORLD VIEW

Continental Europe already regards multi-disciplinary practices as a fact of life, and in France, for instance, accountants KPMG own the largest firm of lawyers in the country. In Britain the Law Society still prohibits mergers between legal and non-legal firms, although since 1988 solicitors have been allowed to associate with non-lawyers, provided they do not share fees.

Thus international accountants such as Arthur Andersen, Price Waterhouse and most recently, Coopers and Lybrand, have well publicised associations with one law firm in particular: they are respectively, Garrett & Co. (headed by Arthur Andersen's former in-house lawyer, Colin Garrett), Arnheim & Co, and Stephenson and Harwood.

Representatives of 20 middle-sized British legal firms which met with the President of the Law Society earlier this year believe that, rather than resist what is inevitable, they should draft regulation to govern such practices. The Labour Party and the Office of Fair Trading have made it clear that they want an end to what they see as restrictive practice.

Those British lawyers who object to such mergers do so because they believe it could lead to a conflict of professional and business interests. Senior partner John Clitheroe says: "The desire for one-stop shopping, accountancy and legal services together, is hard to resist. But I have major objections to it because the ethos of accounting is different from the ethos of legal practice – not less honourable, but based on different considerations."

It is not only the multi-nationals which are influencing changes in legal attitudes. Entrepreneurial American companies, especially within the IT industry, are having a radical impact. Lawyer John Osborn, author of 'The Paperchase' and 'The Associates,' says: "The law school mentality is that in order to have a valid contract, you have got to meet all these legal requirements. But the business guys are now saying, 'Well, to hell with it then, we won't have a valid contract. Think about it. What's more important to us – selling our machines or listening to you?' So the next lawyer walks in and agrees to come up with a three-page contract."

He cites as an example one company that specialises in producing highly complex computer equipment for which it might receive a bulk order every five or six months. "The lawyers they used to have would raise all sorts of objections, which made drawing up the contracts so difficult that it took six months to close a deal, and sales slowed down. What's more, the guys who were selling this equipment never knew what the contracts meant anyway. So they said, 'Goodbye, we're going to get somebody else'. These lawyers were costing them too much money."

Consequently, there is now emerging a counter-model to the eastern seaboard New York lawyer and law firm, whose personality has traditionally dominated legal practice in the US. This 'new age' breed, says Osborn, consider themselves, first and foremost, 'transactional lawyers', part of the business team. "They are present to assist and conduct the transaction, whether it be a venture capital agreement, an IPO (Initial Public Offering), or a simple incorporation involving three guys who say, 'I've had it with the big company. We're going to start our own little venture here'."

Lawyers, especially those in California, where they are reputed to number around

Californian lawyer, Henry Hecht

Lawyers

140,000 (second only to Washington DC, and its Government lawyers), happen to be living in a most interesting evolutionary period of US law, according to Osborn. Wilson Sonsini Goodrich and Rosati, he says, is the fastest growing law firm in Silicon Valley. The offices, set in parkland near Palo Alto, resemble a college campus and have names like 'Tahoe' and 'Sequoia'. "What I like about it is that for the first time, you've got a California-personality law firm. How much more pleasant it must be to be work in a two-storey office that looks like a pseudo Frank Lloyd Wright building and relates to its environment, instead of a skyscraper.

"I'll give you a tip: In the next ten years, unless these lawyers are going to court, they will be wearing jeans to work and at partners' meetings; everybody's door will be open, and they'll be drinking cappuccino in the lounge. It will be a world away from the wood-panelled environment of Wall Street and private clubs where the associates get to go if they have been good boys and girls."

"The high-technology industry is the fastest growing area for lawyers because companies are constantly breaking off each other and regrouping in different ways. And it's interesting that this kind of business is transforming the culture of the law firm. The lawyers have come to reflect the clients they represent; a guy coming from the Microsoft campus in Seattle would feel right at home."

In one radical case, which Osborn views as part of a developing trend, a business that fired its old-established legal practice was not content merely to go out and hire a 'new age' law firm; it opted instead to train some of its own people as in-house lawyers. "The view was, 'We're not going to go all the way and hire a law firm that looks like us. We'll just make the guys we've got, who are like us, lawyers'."

But while the mood in the West may increasingly give way to those characteristics long associated with the US – expediency and the pursuit of the fast buck – it is tempered by the universal fear of a malpractice (negligence) suit. Dissatisfied clients on both sides of the Atlantic are now more likely to sue a law firm, which can then turn round and sue the negligent lawyer.* "If you want to terrify someone in my office, you just say, 'Lister v Romford Ice'," says American lawyer, Dan Soffin, who practises as a British solicitor, referring to a case which established an employer's right to sue an employee.

US attorney, Madelyn Chaber, says: "American lawyers get sued all the time, but it is not common that the complaint goes anywhere. What generally brings it about is that the client is not satisfied with the result. However, even if it is a bad result, it is not necessarily because the lawyer did anything wrong. There are also times when a case will fall between the cracks, a deadline is missed, say, and that's why lawyers have malpractice insurance."

The desire to minimise one's liability in the case of a malpractice suit has led to an emphasis on measuring and checking which never stops. In the US, 'backing up the

---

* Barristers cannot be sued by their clients for negligence in court or in preparation of court work but their immunity does not extend to negligent advice.

back-up' is simply a matter of course.

"American lawyers are much more aggressive at finding the facts of each individual case," says one international lawyer. The massive discovery system that has been generated is a result of that. For example, in the UK, if you wanted to know whether an insurance premium was fair, you would talk to an underwriter, to the broker. In the US, lawyers would ask for the discovery of every single premium that had ever been paid on this particular policy, and then they would ask for premiums on other policies, and finally they would ask for premiums with other insurers. They would build a picture to show, objectively and substantively, whether the premium was fair."

BRITISH TREND

He is not alone in his conviction that more and more of these expensive American practices will become a standard part of British law. In some of London's leading firms they have already been incorporated. "On city transactions like corporate project finance, you must have back-up information to prove everything that is sent to you is correct. Absolutely everything is checked and logged," says a corporate lawyer. "Any case which goes to court has masses of background information, you wouldn't believe how much, which can entail a junior finding and filing documents, full-time."

While malpractice suits are on the increase, lawsuits in the US are down. California attorney Chaber says there is a mistaken assumption, at home as well as abroad, that anyone at all sues on every imaginable pretext, and plaintiffs reap enormous rewards. "If you question people when you are choosing a jury and ask, 'How many people think there is an excessive number of lawsuits?', everyone's hand goes up. But California statistics show that the number of lawsuits has been declining in the past ten years.

"And if you asked people which type of cases are crowding the courts, they would say personal injury, product liability. But those are less than ten per cent of all lawsuits filed in the state. Most cases concern companies. They do not involve individuals at all. For example, the most recent case of punitive damages being awarded involved two companies one of which was ordered by the court to pay the other $26 million.

"Furthermore, if you ask people for an example of a frivolous law suit, an unfair verdict, they'll bring up the case in which an 81 year old woman was awarded $2.9 million because she spilled coffee she had bought at McDonald's and was horribly

US attorney, Madelyn Chaber

burned. What they do not take into account is, first, the judge reduced the amount and, secondly, McDonald's had received at least 700 reports of coffee burns ranging from mild to third degree, and had settled claims arising from scalding injuries for more than $500,000. Even so, McDonald's stood by its economic decision to keep their coffee that hot so it could sit, ready to be served, and not have to be re-made so often."

WRITTEN CONSTITUTION

Robert Post, US Professor of Law at Berkeley, says America is a particularly litigious society because, "for one thing, we have so little binding us in the way of customary traditions that we have developed legal ways of evolving everything." Based on a written Constitution, US law is also more tolerant of interpretation and transformation than law in Britain.

"In England," says Post, "the appellate court will look at precedent and say, 'This is the law', as though they've 'found' something. The attitude is that the law is a given; it is in the decisions, it is in the books, there is little choice. A judge there will say, 'What do the precedents require?', whereas in America a judge will say, 'Now, what is the right policy decision and in that light I will interpret the precedent'. This judicial responsiveness to currents of opinion creates the climate in which legal action is encouraged."

And the financial rewards for the legal profession ensure the continuation of such a climate. "People are influenced by the fact that if you can get into a good law school and do OK, you can make $90,000 right off the bat. And they are right, they can, " says lawyer, John Osborn. "I would be willing to bet that not one student out of an entire class at Stanford (Law School) desires to be a criminal defence attorney. Believe me, they would love to be the lawyer for, say, Silicon Graphics which buys eight small companies a month, each time generating a nice bunch of cash."

This is corroborated by New York attorney Neal Johnston, who recalled a law professor saying, "None of you will ever practise criminal law, because Harvard men long ago learned that crime does not pay."

RICHER THAN 'HECK'

The prizes are great for those who possess the marketing skills (legal ability is taken as read) and sheer physical stamina, lawyer Henry Hecht says: "A corporate lawyer might bill 2,500 hours in a year and he will work many more hours than he bills," but the earnings will be huge. At the most successful American firms, profits per partner can dwarf those at the most profitable firms in Britain, climbing to the equivalent of six, seven, or eight hundred thousand pounds a year.

At such élite firms, standards are maintained by ruthless self-policing. But, attorney Madelyn Chaber says: "I know some plaintiff lawyers who are horrible lawyers and are richer than heck, driving around in Rolls Royces - so it can be a lucrative profession. You don't even have to be doing a good job and you can make a lot of money."

The success of such lawyers is due to pursuing the

right issue at the right time, with the right client. Corporations have had to pay millions of dollars to plaintiffs, whether individuals or groups in a 'class-action' suit, who have been harmed by their products or pollution. "The huge Dow Chemical Company, for instance, which survived a decade of protest over its manufacture of defoliants for use in the Vietnam war, was nearly bankrupted by lawsuits over its silicone breast implants."

The desire to win is paramount. Professor Post says: "If you are a contingency lawyer, you need to win to live. Settling can be winning too, because if you are a litigator it enables you to bring in the money without the expenses of a trial. Winning means getting the right result which is very different from the 'Perry Mason' ideal."

The US system of law is one in which everyone pays his own lawyer and, with a few exceptions, the losing side does not pay the winning side's costs. Consequently, contrary to public perception, it has long been acknowledged by the profession, says John Osborn, that apart from huge class-action suits, "it's suicide ever to go to court in America."

"A lawsuit is like a sickness. Your lawyer has essentially failed if you go to court. It is the most expensive, crazy option to take. In our law firm, as soon as we tell our clients that they are not going to court under any circumstances, they loosen up immediately. And I think all business-oriented law firms operate in this way."

While a rich client can afford to pay by the hour, or even up front, such a system penalises virtually everyone else in the US. And so to combat this and make the legal redress of grievances available to all (in theory at least), contingency fees were introduced. Under this arrangement, a lawyer is allowed to take a case on the basis that his fee will be a percentage of the winnings.

ADVERTISING

Contingency fees have provoked a mixture of genuine concern, snobbery and a plethora of bold, brash and often absurd advertising in the 'Yellow Pages', on TV and radio. Osborn speaks for many when he says, "If you are using a lawyer in the Yellow Pages, you're in trouble already."

Hecht, however, says that while such lawyers may have the lowest status in the profession, they may be providing a useful service. "You could make a very strong argument that they empower people who would not otherwise have any idea of their legal rights."

Fellow academic Robert Post, agrees. "Clearly, a lawyer who goes into a hospital room where there is an injured person (to solicit business) is crossing the line. But some-one who inserts an ad. may be extending the availability of the law. How he does it may seem tasteless and offen-sive to the Bar, who want to think of themselves as a worthy profession, and above that kind of advertising, but I think it is very easy to get on one's high horse and be judgmental."

He admits, however, that the US does not have 'very good mechanisms' for choosing lawyers and strongly advocates that the Bar provide consumer reports. "Consumers should have access to evaluations about law firms and what complaints there are, if any. But the profession is not willing to open this process to the public."

Arguably the most contentious aspect of American law, however, is the way in which lawyers calculate and collect their contingency fees. On the one hand, limiting the amount a lawyer can charge may limit his ability to bring a lawsuit; on the other, if his fee is too high, it can be an abuse. In February this year, a law firm in Savannah, Georgia, won a $4.8 million malpractice suit against a hospital after their client, Julia Mae Shiggs slipped into an irreversible coma, and lawyers David Roberson and John Woodall, were alleged to have extracted 72 per cent of her money.

The normal share is a third, in complicated or trial cases, 40%. What attracted the judge's wrath was not the lawyers taking a 50% fee, not illegal, but the way the final bill had been calculated. By adding on notional elements for hypothetical future medical care, it was decided an additional $1.4 million should be added to the original $3.4 million cash award.

According to court documents, the 50% was based on this total, and cheques were written for $2.4 million in fees and more for expenses, apparently without court approval.

The case was referred to the Court of Appeal, where a judgment has yet to be made on the amount to which the attorneys will be entitled. But to avoid penalising the client by this delay, the court made arrangements for the guardian of Shiggs' children to access the money.

The Future

No discussion of law in America would be complete, of course, without mention of the O.J. Simpson trial. Unanimously described by the US lawyers interviewed for this chapter as 'a circus', it was condemned as the most notorious example of the way money and publicity can vulgarise and distort the conduct of a serious case.

"Justice was not served by that trial and it has caused tremendous harm to the public's perception of the law and lawyers," says Chaber. "We rate somewhere below funeral undertakers and used-car salesmen. I've seen changes in the people out there – there is such cynicism about the legal system now.

"Jurors feel as if they are being asked to perform some horrible task, that it is a punishment rather than a privilege of a democratic society. In my last trial, jury selection involved interviewing fifteen panels of between 70 and 80 people before we found twelve whom we felt could be fair. The rest were so jaded, so cynical and so turned off. The judge was shocked."

Nonetheless, many US lawyers, including Chaber, support the idea of televised trials in principle so that, in more mundane cases, the public is able to see the way the legal system actually works, rather than relying on a fictionalised viewpoint. Such possible educational benefits, they realise, are considerably diminished by the choice of cases, which blatantly appeals to the curious and the prurient.

In one week on the Courtroom Television Network, US, viewers could choose between a case of a woman afraid of heights who confessed to manslaughter after police

Lawyers

detectives took her to a 300-foot clifftop, and a battle between rock singer Jerry Garcia's widow and a former wife over royalties for music, menswear and cherry ice cream.

Thus it is not surprising that some lawyers such as Post would like to see the removal of courtroom cameras in celebrity cases, "where there is no pressing need for the public to see it, only prurient interest."

OKLAHOMA

TV cameras are banned from federal courtrooms. It is somewhat ironic that their absence was one of the reasons given for the efficient handling of the Oklahoma City bombing trial. The original 12 jurors in the trial remained intact, and deliberated over four days, before convicting Timothy McVeigh in the bombing that killed 168 people.

"I think everyone, including the defence, was looking over their shoulder at O.J.," * said John Walsh, a former federal prosecutor in Denver. "The judge kept both sides focused on what really was evidence and the absence of cameras helped keep lawyers in check. It wasn't entertainment in the way that televised high-profile trials have been where all the parties, including the judge and the witnesses, behaved differently for the cameras."

---

* Simpson's criminal trial lasted almost a year during which 10 members of the jury were replaced for various indiscretions. His acquittal was reached in under four hours.

But equally, the First Amendment of the Constitution*
and the Freedom of Information Act enshrine America's
basic belief that its people have a right to know – and
nowhere was this more clearly demonstrated than in
Watergate which brought down President Nixon. Hecht, a
former Assistant Special Watergate prosecutor, recalls:
"Watergate was a TV phenomenon too and generated the
belief that lawyers are able to do good, they prosecute
bad people.

"I am sure you could find statistics which subsequently show there was a big jump in law school admissions,
even though it emerged that many of those involved in
Watergate were also lawyers, which could have led to the
same kind of public scepticism about lawyers as was
displayed towards politicians."

But in the US, public memory is short. "A number of
my students were born the year Nixon resigned in 1974
or the years after his resignation, and so Watergate is
somewhat of an anachronism for many of them. People
are much more focused on current issues. Where before
they might have said 'the lessons of Watergate', now they
are more likely to say 'the lessons of Whitewater'.

"At one level there is some heightened awareness. For
instance, Watergate highlighted the problem of campaign
financing but I don't know that there have been any

---

* *"Congress shall make no law… abridging the freedom of
speech , or of the press, or of the right of the people to peace-
ably assemble."*

Lawyers

fundamental changes as a result of Watergate."

Apart from a statute appointing an army of independent prosecutors, and giving a whole new meaning to the word 'gates', Hecht is ambivalent about any lasting impact Watergate may have had on the law and its practitioners today. "I am disappointed by the use of 'gate' as a generic term to denote any scandal or misuse of power. It demeans the importance of the Watergate cases which involved what I would call pervasive misuse of the power of the Presidency."

Clearly, the idealistic vision that many lawyers held in Hecht's day has given way to a much more materialistic one. A poll conducted by 'The National law Journal' on 'What America Really Thinks About Lawyers, a decade before the O.J Simpson trial, revealed that, even then, lawyers were regarded as greedy. The second and third reasons for disapproval of lawyers were that lawyers, 'manipulate the legal system without any concern for right or wrong,' and they 'file too many unnecessary lawsuits'.

Yet when the public was asked what were the most positive aspects of lawyers, the most popular responses were that their 'first priority is to their clients' and that they 'know how to cut through bureaucratic red tape'.

An earlier survey by the American Bar Foundation concluded bluntly that, although members of the public scorn the image of the 'shyster', they also 'indicated that when they do seek a lawyer, they may want one who most fits the shyster image'.

Professor Robert Post who analysed these profoundly

contradictory attitudes towards lawyers, wrote: "Lawyers are applauded for following their clients' wishes and bending the rules to satisfy those wishes; and they are at the very same time condemned for using the legal system to satisfy their clients' desires by bringing lawsuits at their clients' behest and using the legal system to get what their clients want, rather than to uphold the right and denounce the wrong."

Justice, it would appear, is governed by one's circumstances. There is no absolute – not in this world anyway. A lawyer cannot be expected to serve up justice neatly embodied in law (unless his name is Perry Mason) but is it asking too much of the lack-lustre bulk of the profession to get its act together and deliver a good quality legal service? If it does not, the chilling prospect awaits us in which our right to good legal representation becomes the prerogative of the few: companies and corporations, wealthy individuals and those accused of truly heinous crimes.

THEM AND US

The Louise Woodward case spectacularly highlights a long history of mutual suspicion and antagonism bordering on hostility between two nations divided by a common legal system. Ironically it is because America and Britain share the same legal roots – the US system of Justice is based on English common law – that the differences seem all the more incomprehensible and aggravating.

Despite Britain's less than stainless reputation in the

Lawyers

justice stakes there remains an innate belief by its inhabitants that it possesses the best legal system in the world which explains why there is such a high level of public scepticism about the chances of a British subject obtaining a fair trial abroad.

The conviction of 19-year-old Louise Woodward for the murder of baby Matthew Eappen in a foreign court was confirmation of this country's worst fears and provoked an extraordinary national reaction. Outrage at the court verdict was followed by Woodward supporters from all over Britain descending on her home village of Elton to join in round-the-clock vigils protesting her innocence.

Across the Atlantic, America staunchly maintains that it took the best of the English legal system and improved it by attaching the Constitution. It resents and rejects what it perceives as patronising criticism by the British of its democratic trial system.

Michael Elliott, editor of the International Editions of Newsweek wrote: "Trials like that of Louise Woodward contribute to a misunderstanding of a nation that the rest of the world thinks it knows, but often doesn't."

While the OJ Simpson case highlighted the faults in the objectivity of the US jury system, Americans continue to view it in the same way they view the Presidency. Both are sacrosanct, for they enshrine America's paramount principle of government 'of the people by the people and for the people'.

The Constitution guarantees juries the freedom to judge without interference. Consequently, US judges appear to take a back seat in British eyes because they are not allowed to sum up the evidence at the end of the trial, only the law.

In Britain, where trial by jury is not an inalienable right and the number of civil juries is negligible, the opposite is true. Increasingly, judges are wresting verdicts from the juries and overturning them at Appeal Court level.

The similarities between the English and American criminal justice systems far exceed their differences though. Both share the adversarial system which was developed in the 8th century, coinciding with the rise of lawyers and aggressive lawyering.

England exported the adversarial system to all its colonies but in America aggressive lawyering was taken to extremes and spawned such elaborate rules that the due process of law is now very complicated. A consequence of this is that a trial which would last, say, six hours in the UK would be likely to run for six weeks in California. The irony is that 90% of these US cases are finally resolved in a matter of minutes by a legally enforceable plea-bargain, agreed by the prosecution and defence attorneys, and approved by the judge.

In Britain, Prime Minister Tony Blair's Labour Government clearly has been influenced by American legal practices. To save £300 million, the Lord Chancellor, Lord Irvine intends withdrawing state legal aid for early one million civil cases a year. In future they will be funded through a conditional 'no-win, no-fee' system. Litigants will be expected to take out an insurance policy to cover 'extras' like court costs, though family cases not involving damages claims will still be subsidised.

Lawyers

The plans were presented by the Government as a way of facing down vested interests within the legal profession. Lord Irvine told the Law Society: "Legal aid... must be refocused. It must be a tool to promote access to justice for the needy..."

However, Phillip Sycamore, the Law Society president, said the result would be the opposite: "This cut in access to justice for a large section of society isn't consistent with the goal to create a compassionate Britain."

Further changes were heralded by Home Secretary Jack Straw who threatened to limit the fees of the top earning barristers. "The system at the top end is frankly out of control, he told a meeting of lawyers. "We have to get a grip on the fees, otherwise the system will be so expensive it will grind to a halt. I think there is wide recognition amongst the Bar that the situation cannot go on as now. The days in which lawyers, and especially the criminal Bar, could simply apply upward pressure on the 'going rate' and catapult themselves into ever-higher earnings must end."

These far-reaching reforms will ultimately mean the demise of the legal profession as we have come to know it, and the survival of the individual lawyer will undoubtedly depend upon how swiftly he or she is able to find a profitable specialism and a space in an already overcrowded workplace. Redefining the role of the lawyer is likely to be the single most pressing issue in the decades to come. Many traditional lawyers' tasks have disappeared and still more are destined for virtual extinction. The profession is well and truly 'on the spot'.

Index

Index

Index

Index

Index

Index

Books from Vision

An extract from
THE MILLENNIUM BOMB
Countdown to a £400 Billion Catastrophe
by Simon Reeve and Colin McGhee

...Consider what will happen when we pass through 1999 towards the year 2000. If computers are shortening the date, their clocks will tell them it is the year 99. The next year is therefore the year 00. As millions of people around the globe party the night away on New Years Eve 1999, computer clocks will be happily ticking away, running our modern society and controlling everything from traffic lights and life-support machines to pension payments and missile controls. But as they tick past midnight many of the computers – up to 90% according to some estimates – will start to malfunction. Some will think they have been tampered with and shut-down, while the majority will assume it represents the year 1900, the beginning of the twentieth century, and calculate dates accordingly.

As dawn breaks on New Year's Day over New Zealand and the rest of the South Pacific – the first area of the world to enter the new millennium – some experts warn that up to 50,000 mainframe computers around the world could be at risk of serious malfunction, a wonderful euphemism for shut-down, close or stop. Others warn that nearly everything containing a micro-processor will be at risk.

The potential for economic chaos is enormous. Many experts admit they are being conservative when they estimate that between one and five per cent of businesses could collapse because of the millennium bomb problem. Others have predicted that as many as 50 per cent of companies will not have fixed their computers and will in consequence face catastrophe.

Books from Vision

The science of chaos theory teaches us what happens with a ripple effect, like a single drop of water falling into a still pond: the effects can be felt around the entire pond as tiny ripples spread across the surface. Chaos theory also teaches us that a butterfly flapping its wings in South America causes storms in Europe: the tiny creature is the start of a chain reaction that alters global events. And so it is with this minor computer glitch.

We believe the problem is much more serious than current thinking suggests, but even if we accept the estimate that perhaps only one per cent of businesses will fail, it will still be enough to cause a sudden economic crisis. The doomed businesses will all fail within a very short space of time, and as they collapse so their supply companies, clients and everyone else upstream and downstream in their chain of business will be harmed.

Those wondering how a simple date could cause any significant problems, the sort that affect daily life and routine, should consider how computers govern our lives. The humble traffic light is controlled by a computer which tells it when to turn green, amber and red. The length of time it allocates for each lane or road of traffic to pass through on green is decided according to a carefully formulated program imbedded deep within the computer which switches between the various colours according to the day of the week. Sometimes traffic going into town during rush-hour is given more green lights than at other times of the day or at the weekend. If the computer controlling traffic lights cannot tell the day of the week correctly it cannot operate properly and direct the flow of traffic: 'gridlock'.

But computers control much more than traffic lights. The millennium bomb could mean that your building society might generously add '99' years of interest to your high-interest savings account. Unfortunately at the same time your bank may start charging 99 years of interest on your mortgage. Prison computers might suddenly calculate that murderers and rapists are eligible for parole having served considerably longer sentences than foreseen by the judge who appears to have convicted them '99' years previously.

Every computer will react differently, but tests that are already being conducted by companies desperate to find a cure for the glitch have proved that many computers will simply work out the difference in years between 1999 and 1900 and calculate a giant leap of 99 years. Even the most advanced computer is only as good as the person or people who programmed it, and in many cases that could have been as many as a thousand programmers, each of them tapping away for several years to create their own tiny part.

A computer runs many different software applications to do a variety of tasks, and each of these applications may involve many programs. All of them, like the programmers, are cogs, without any understanding of the full workings of the rest of their joint creation. With so many people needed to mesh together to create a highly technical system, it is hardly surprising that mistakes are made and glitches go unnoticed.

Worse, it is much more difficult to go back through it all and cure the problems, which is one of the main reasons for the appalling lack of action taken by computer companies in the years, and even decades, since this problem became known. Until recently computer companies made no attempt to purge the machines they were supplying to industry and the public of the glitch. The result of this, probably the most costly and ridiculous error in history, is now troubling leaders of governments and industry...

Books from Vision

An extract from
POWER AND CORRUPTION
The Rotten Core of Government and Big Business
by Stephen Moore

...It is the sort of situation which would warrant the immediate despatch of James Bond 007 – an idyllic island in the Caribbean is taken over by a sinister criminal organisation.

In one of Ian Fleming's novels it would have been the evil organisation SPECTRE which seizes control. Bond would have despatched the villains with the help of a Walther PPK, a gorgeous girl on his arm and a vodka martini at the bar.

Yet the reality in the 1990s is just as dramatic.

The beautiful Caribbean island of Aruba, only five miles wide and 20 miles long, was 'bought' by elements of the Sicilian Mafia along with its 65,000 inhabitants. Everything of importance on the island was taken over by the mobsters, controlling elements of the police, politicians, customs and, most importantly, the banks. The 'ownership' of their own State offered wonderful opportunities for corruption on a previously unthinkable scale. Its very existence was founded on corruption and criminality.

Aruba lies just off the Venezuelan coast. During the age of discovery and conquest it was ignored by the Spanish, who described it as 'barren and useless', despite its beautiful long white beaches, and instead it fell into the hands of the Dutch and became part of the six Dutch Antilles.

Sleepy and ignored it was the perfect off-shore Shangri-La for the Mafia. For years they kept their ownership quiet, transforming Aruba into a staging post for cocaine smuggling. At the same time they bribed officials and used the island's banks to launder their money - channelling vast sums obtained from drug dealing, extortion, murder and prostitution across the world.

The authorities only discovered the Mafia's presence after a dramatic and violent police raid on offices in Caracas, the capital of Venezuela. Investigators seized computer disks concerning deals involving the Cuntreras family, one of the most dangerous Sicilian Mafia clans. The Cuntreras had been living in Venezuela for years and visiting Aruba for lengthy holidays. But the disks and other documents showed they had been doing more in the Caribbean than soaking up the sun.

The information seized by the police proved that more than 60% of businesses and economic life on Aruba was owned and controlled by the Mafia.

When the American authorities belatedly realised what was going on there was little they could do. One of their most expensive satellites was moved off course to 'sit' on top of the island and spot smugglers boats and cocaine drops in the ocean, but it was a difficult task even when the clouds allowed vision. One of the largest hauls of cocaine ever discovered in Britain came via Aruba.

Investigators came to the conclusion that the Mafia wanted Aruba not only to create the perfect base for corruption and crime, but also as a bolt-hole they could flee to when they needed to escape the law and avoid extradition to America, Europe or, more specifically, Italy.

Their fears soon seemed justified. In September 1992 Venezuela agreed to extradite back to Italy three of the most dangerous Cuntreras brothers: Guiseppe, Pasquale and Paulo, a trio known as the Black Emperors and reputedly worth more than $1 billion each, earned from drugs. Back home they were arrested and thrown into Italy's top-security Pianosa prison.

Investigators claim the Black Emperors took part in the appalling murder of Judge Giovanni Falcone, who was blown up shortly after he arranged for their extradition to Italy. They then assassinated Paulo Borsellino, Falcone's successor.

According to the US Drug Enforcement Agency the Cuntreras were the main force behind the acquisition of Aruba, a buying spree which started in the early 1980s, when the Black Emperors were frequent visitors to the island with their 'beautiful' wives. They stayed at first in Spartan accommodation, were kind to their kids and avoided ostentatious displays of wealth, according to locals. Meanwhile they were arranging the purchase of restaurants, banks, hotels, cafés, and every type of local business.

Organised crime was hardly a newcomer to the region. From the arrival of pirates and buccaneers centuries ago to the more recent arrivals of fugitive financiers and money launderers, every criminal wants a home in the Caribbean. The island was quick to welcome the latest arrivals with their new investment and the Aruba government took little action, perhaps through fear of reprisals. Exceptionally, one member of the gang was arrested in 1988 and the Aruban authorities requested military assistance from Holland as protection. The Dutch took the request seriously and sent a frigate and a force of soldiers.

The Aruba experience shows that while the Mafia's global power has been under attack, the income from organised crime, the ability to hide it, to launder it and the ability to use it for corruption still poses great threats to international order...

Books from Vision

An extract from
GANGSTA
The Sinister Spread of Yardie Gun Culture
by John Davison

"IT'S the youth, man, it's the youth. All they're interested in is money, trainers, cars and pussy. Education is too slow for them, even a job is too slow. They want it now."

The speaker is Gilly, a huge 'dred' (Rastafarian) DJ, who has just finished his early hours set at the Frontline 'blues', an illegal music and drinking club. Reggae sounds continue to pound out through wreaths of ganja smoke and exclusively black heads nod sagely to the beat, as we cram into a relatively quiet corner of the kitchen to eat goat curry and put the world to rights. Gilly is talking about the state of affairs in his own community of Handsworth, Birmingham. But just as the 'blues' scene could easily be taking place in parts of London, Bristol or Nottingham, his bleak view could equally be a description of life in many areas of inner-city Britain, 1997.

Standing at about six-foot-five, at least half as wide across the shoulders and with a resplendent mane of rasta 'locks', Gilly is not a man you would wish to argue with anyway. His opinion, however, has a personal, tragic context to add to its weight. Days before our conversation he had seen his eldest son, 19, sentenced to 12 years imprisonment on robbery and drugs charges.

"He's been locked up before, and I told him he would have to settle down. But he wouldn't listen," says Gilly, who is 36, with a dismissive shrug. Another one bites the dust.

From elsewhere in the kitchen come other contributions about the delinquent tendencies of the local 'yout'. "We got all kinds of gangs, all kind of crews," says Shelley,

Books from Vision

the man on the pans. "There's the Burger Bar crew, now. They're into drugs and stealing cars. Then there's that bunch of girls who stuck up a bus."

A bus? Girls? "Yeah, man. They stick up a bus with knives and rob everybody on it," says another grey-hair, laughing in spite of himself. "Like a fucking stagecoach robbery."

Later that very day, as chance would have it, a youth – said to be a leading light of the Burger Bar crew – was arrested after police raided his house in Handsworth and found two firearms with ammunition, £30,000 worth of 'crack' cocaine and large bundles of cash. On Sunday of the same weekend the local Post Office was robbed and left boarded up. Locals would now have to travel further afield in order to 'check their books' for benefit money. "Soon we'll have nothing left in Handsworth," said a Frontline regular, staring down the Soho Road the day after.

Back in the kitchen, at about 4am on Saturday morning, and Gilly offers to take me 'on the road' to visit some other kicking (and illegal) night-spots..

One, of two knocked-together former council houses, opens up like the Tardis to reveal a very organised operation. Two large, ram-full rooms accommodate music and dancing with the kitchen and bar serving from the middle. Gilly taps a blind wall to another room. "That's where the gambling goes on," he says.

He has to shout above the gut-shaking bass thump of Jamaican music. One growling rapper is singing the praises of gun power, along the lines of: "If you hafna' got a gun, you got nuttin' to say roun' here." Another, although backed by an equally aggressive rhythm, is appealing for 'Respec' to be shown to women.

Outside, as we leave, a group of predominantly white prostitutes shivers on the pavement under the watchful eye of their black minder.

Another blues, or 'shabeen', is accommodated in a single terraced house. It is alarmingly full, including the precipitous staircase, and the only man with room to move is the DJ who operates in the corner of the main room behind metal grilles.

A third is in an innocent looking bungalow on a residential street. A group of youths are huddled round the entrance. "You see them guys?" says Gilly as we approach. "They're bound to be dealing something."

Inside, elegantly word-processed notices on the wall say: "BEWARE MUGGERS. People leaving this club have been mugged. Be careful." Welcome to the ghetto.

This is a strange, alien world which most people in Britain never see. To my personal shame, I worked as a journalist in Birmingham for two years in the 1980's and never came close. It is not without its attractions. But Handsworth, and places like it, have been the crucible of frightening changes over the past few years which are of profound importance to society as a whole.

The gun and 'gun-play' is now the hard currency on these streets. It was brought by the Yardies, say locals, and their own youth has adopted it with enthusiasm. Things are predicted to get a lot worse before they get any better.

Since the summer of 1995, the area has seen five murders, at least six attempted murders and numerous other shootings by gunmen. Guns are openly worn in public, and policemen have been threatened at gun-point. Local officers fear that it is only a matter of time before one of them is shot dead in the course of their duty.

Books from Vision

THE MILLENNIUM BOMB - Countdown to a £400 billion Catastrophe by Simon Reeve and Colin McGhee
This is the first general interest book in the world to investigate the infamous year 2000 problem which could herald a global economic disaster. Computers may fail if they cannot cope with the new date when the clocks tick past midnight on December 31st 1999. Missile systems may shut down, stock market trading systems could crash and every type of business may be crippled. Almost anything with a computer chip - from virtual pets to vital life-saving health equipment is at risk and the authors ask - how prepared are governments to deal with this impending crisis? THE MILLENNIUM BOMB has received high-profile publicity since its release in 1997 - from the Times Literary Supplement to Channel 4 news, The BBC World Service to The Evening Standard (London).
ISBN: 1-901250-00-8

INSTRUMENTS OF TERROR - Mass Destruction has Never Been So Easy by Dr Frank Barnaby
Terrorism has become an unstoppable threat. INSTRUMENTS OF TERROR explains how renegade groups could soon obtain and detonate a weapon of mass destruction. The increased availability of information over the Internet has made it possible for individuals or groups to cause carnage on an unprecedented scale - even a child could find out how to build a devastating weapon by cruising the net. Following the breakdown of the Soviet Union, the materials needed to build a crude nuclear bomb have never been so easy to obtain. Dr Frank Barnaby also warns of the threat of cyber-terrorism: weapons which destroy a nations infrastructure by attacking critical computer systems.
ISBN: 1-901250-01-6

Books from Vision

**GANGSTA - The Sinister Spread of Yardie Gun Culture
by John Davison**
A man intervenes in a row at an illegal drinking den. He is shot
four times and left for dead. A woman argues with a crack
dealer. She is marched up three flights of stairs, beaten over the
head and thrown from the window.
This is the reality of life among the Yardie criminals who have
exploded out of Jamaica to spread crack cocaine, guns and
death across the West. The author, an award winning journalist,
spent years researching this book, during which time he uniquely
gained the support of both the gangstas and the police who
were investigating them. He graphically describes stories of
killing, torture, drug-dealing, shoot-outs
and bungled police raids.
ISBN: 1-901250-02-4

**POWER AND CORRUPTION - The Rotten Core
of Government and Big Business by Stephen Moore**
An epidemic of corruption is tainting politics and trade across
the globe. POWER AND CORRUPTION reveals there are major
scandals in almost every country which the police are powerless
to prevent. The author questions the morality of major companies
where pay-offs and kick-backs are an accepted method of clinch-
ing a deal and he also asks why so few people are prepared to
stop the worst excesses. The author, an Oxford educated police
detective, analyses why police forces and governments do not
have the capacity to tackle corruption; his disturbing conclusion
is that governments lack the will to stop the rot.
ISBN: 1-901250-03-2

Books from Vision

**THE PLAGUE MAKERS - The Secret World of
Biological Warfare by Wendy Barnaby**
New strains of superbug are a frightening threat, and this is no
accident of nature. Viruses are being specially engineered in the
laboratory to spread death and disease
- including new forms of plague.
Many say that no country would ever dare unleash such a terror
as a means of waging war but THE PLAGUE MAKERS uncovers
disturbing evidence of military experimentation.
Some countries and some terrorist groups are exploiting the
latest advances in genetic engineering.
The author delves back into the past to reveal previous germ
warfare atrocities. We learn that under apartheid, South Africa
was one of the most advanced germ warfare regimes, funding
the work by manufacturing drugs like Ecstasy.
The fear is that many other countries are building an arsenal
using easily accessible scientific know-how. The book questions
whether scientists and politicians can be trusted, concluding that
many are complacent about the all-too-real danger.
ISBN: 1-901250-04-0

ACID - The Secret History of LSD
TOBACCO WARS - The Immoral Earnings of the Cigarette
Industry
BIG BROTHER IS TAXING YOU! - Can We Trust The
Inland Revenue?
WOUNDED TIGER - Freedom Fighting is Big Business
THE NEW EMPERORS - The Power of Organised Crime
DIRTY BUSINESS - Who Plays Fair in the Boardroom?
THE WOMAN FROM MOSSAD - The Torment of
Mordechai Vanunu
SECRET CULT - The School of Economic Science Mystery
I-SPY - The Black Art of Bugging
SEX SYMBOLS

VISION INVESTIGATION SERIES Order Form

If you have enjoyed this book and would be interested in any other Vision Investigations, you can order directly from the publisher (UK only). Full details of existing and forthcoming titles can be found on the preceding pages.
All titles are £10.00 *including* postage and packaging.

The Millennium Bomb . . . .___ copies
Instruments of Terror . . . .___ copies
Gangsta . . . . .___ copies
Power and Corruption . . . ___ copies
The Plague Makers . . . . . ___ copies
Lawyers on the Spot . . . . ___ copies
ACID . . . . .___ copies
Tobacco Wars . . . . ___ copies

Big Brother is Taxing You! ___ copies
Wounded Tiger . . . . ___ copies
The New Emperors . . . . . .___ copies
Dirty Business . . . . .___ copies
Woman From Mossad . . .___ copies
Secret Cult . . . . .___ copies
I-Spy . . . . .___ copies
Sex Symbols . . . . ___ copies

Total number of books ordered:. . . . . _____copies

Total cost: (£10.00 per book). . . . .£_____

Name . . . .
Address . . . .
. . . .
Post Code. . . . . .Telephone. . . . .
Mastercard, Visa, Amex, Diners accepted
Please specify card type:. . . . .
Card No:. . . . . .Expiry date: . . . ./. . . . .
Or I enclose a cheque made payable to Vision Paperbacks

Signature:. . . . .
Please allow 28 days delivery
If you have any queries, please call our orders hotline on:
0171 323 9757 Fax: 0171 323 9747

VISION Paperbacks
20 Queen Anne Street
London W1M 0AY